The
Celtic Songlines

Línte Ceoil Cheiltigh

with
Dónal Lunny

David Forsythe

Línte Ceoil Cheiltigh

The Celtic Songlines

Dónal Lunny

ALBAIN
SCOTLAND

ÉIRE
IRELAND

OILEÁN
MHANANN
ISLE OF MAN

BHREATAIN
BHEAG
WALES

CORN NA BREATAINE
CORNWALL

BHRIOTÁIN
BRITTANY

GHAILÍS
GALICIA

ASTÚIRÍS
ASTURIAS

The Celtic Songlines

Línte Ceoil Cheiltigh

with *Dónal Lunny*

David Forsythe

First published in 2017 by Currach Press
23 Merrion Square North, Dublin 2
www.currach.ie

1 2 3 4 5 6 7 8 9 10

ISBN: 978-1-78218-896-4

Set in Avenir and Colmcille

Cover and book design by Bright Idea, Killarney
Project editor Siobhán Prendergast, Dingle Publishing Services
Printed by Walsh Colour Print, Castleisland

ALBAIN
SCOTLAND

ÉIRE
IRELAND

OILEÁN
MHANANN
ISLE OF MAN

BHREATAIN
BHEAG
WALES

CORN NA BREATAINE
CORNWALL

BHRIOTÁIN
BRITTANY

GHAILÍS
GALICIA

ASTÚIRIS
ASTURIAS

Foreword

Is there such a thing as 'Celtic music' and if there is, what exactly is it? These are questions that I sought the answers to when we set about making this four-part musical travelogue series.

For *The Celtic Songlines* we visited the mighty Cliffs of Moher, and journeyed north to my mother's birthplace in Donegal. Back in Dublin we called in to the Irish Traditional Music Archive. Then we set sail for the Celtic nations of Europe, from the Hebrides in the north of Scotland to Galicia in the far south, visiting Scotland itself, the Isle of Man, Wales, Cornwall and Brittany. Along the way we met with musicians, historians and folklorists, who helped build a fascinating picture of what Celtic musical identity means in modern Europe.

At the beginning of the project, I enlisted the help of some of the country's most accomplished musicians and together we went to Grouse Lodge Studios in Westmeath. There, we recorded a number of pieces that were connected to one or other of the places we were to visit. The idea came from the producer/director David Bickley and it proved really useful as a means of weaving the different musical strands together. We brought these recordings with us and added various musicians along the way. I thought it worked out really well.

Some of the best-known folk and traditional musicians in Europe took part in the programme, including the likes of Paddy Glackin, Mairéad Ní Mhaonaigh, Alan Stivell, Donald Shaw, Susana Seivane and Carlos Núñez. For me, meeting and playing with such an exciting variety of musicians all across Europe was a happy and rewarding process.

At the Royal Conservatoire of Scotland in Glasgow we encountered a new generation of traditional musicians that are coming on stream, while on the remote Isle of Canna we were given a rare glimpse of one of the most comprehensive collections of Celtic music and folklore in existence.

Wherever we went we met up with local musicians and basically just played with them and it was a very enjoyable experience. The whole idea of the series – and this book – was to explore the musical and cultural connections between the different Celtic countries. But what really struck me as we went along was that the people themselves were the connection. I had been to many of our destinations before, but in travelling from one region to the next in succession, the qualities that they had in common became more apparent. I became very aware that we are all one scattered tribe, with common roots.

Wherever we went, I felt a genuine empathy with the musicians. The enthusiasm was real and the love for their art was plain to see. This is what united them all. For example, I had always been conscious of the close ties between Scotland and Ireland, but what also came through to me was this great passion for keeping their heritage alive and building on it.

As well as looking at where these traditions have come from, we also looked at where they are likely to be going, talking to young upcoming musicians and artists as well. On the Isle of Skye we met with members of the Peatbog Fairies and on the Isle of Man we were told about the resurgence in Manx traditional music being driven by a new generation of young musicians.

In Brittany I met vibrant chanteuse Kohann and also joined piper Konan Mevel from electro-Celtic band Skilda to play a tune in a neolithic tomb!

The journey took us from north to south along the Atlantic coasts of Europe, visiting some of the continent's most spectacular scenery along the way, reaching our journey's end at the Tower of Hercules in A Coruña on Spain's north west coast. It was from here that the legendary Celtic king Breogán was said to have sighted a verdant green isle to the north and thereupon set sail to settle a new Celtic kingdom.

This journey has been a hugely positive experience overall. The infectious enthusiasm of young musicians inspires great confidence and optimism for the future of our own music, and for all of the traditions from Scotland to Galicia.

Celtic music has developed a cultural identity of its own in recent years, but what really gives it life and unites all these places is the spirit and love that Celtic people have for their own traditions.

Dónal Lunny

Acknowledgements

The Celtic Songlines was devised and produced by David Bickley at Alchemy Electronic Arts

Barbara McCormack, Russell Library, Maynooth University

National Museum of Ireland

Irish Traditional Music Archive

RTÉ

Colm O'Callaghan

Jim Lockhart

Grouse Lodge Studios

Royal Conservatoire of Scotland

Canna House and the National Trust of Scotland

Sabhal Mòr Ostaig

The Old Inn, Carbost, Isle of Skye

House of Manannan

Castle Rushen

Culture Vannin

Llio Rhydderch

Felin Uchaf

Dare Mason at the VIP Lounge

Kings Arms, St Just, Cornwall

Festival Interceltique de Lorient

Konan Mevel

Olivier Agogué, conservateur du patrimoine – chef du Service Départemental d'Archéologie du Morbihan

Obradoiro de Gaitas Seivane

Rodrigo Arbones Bares, Irish College, Santiago De Compostella

Torre de Hércules, A Coruña

Lynch's pub, Miltown Malbay

Paul Coghlan, Made4Design, Dublin

Garry O'Sullivan, Columba Press

Siobhán Prendergast, Dingle Publishing Services

Cathal Cudden, Bright Idea Graphic Design, Killarney

ALBAIN
SCOTLAND

ÉIRE
IRELAND

OILEÁN
MHANANN
ISLE OF MAN

BHREATAIN
BHEAG
WALES

CORN NA BREATAINE
CORNWALL

BRIOTÁIN
BRITTANY

GHAILÍS
GALICIA

ASTÚIRIS
ASTÚRIAS

9

Contents

Introduction

Along the spectacular coasts of the Atlantic, the superhighway of the Celtic world, from Scotland in the north to Spain in the south a thriving culture emerged and prospered. Connected through maritime trade and commerce, these ancient lands stretched for more than 1,000 miles and were the last outposts of a proud culture that once dominated Europe.

Through their language, art and poetry the Celts have left an indelible mark on Europe's western fringe though it is in music that their presence is still most keenly felt to this day.

Through the rich musical traditions of these seemingly disparate lands a new Celtic identity has emerged in Scotland, Ireland, the Isle of Man, Wales, Cornwall, Brittany and northwest Spain.

In 2017, celebrating his 70th year, renowned Irish musician Dónal Lunny embarked on a journey following the Celtic Songlines from the Hebrides to Galicia searching for the connections in history, music and culture that have endured to this day. On his journey Dónal played with some of Europe's most gifted musicians and met with folklorists, musicologists and leading cultural figures.

In this book we trace that journey and investigate the cultural and musical story of the Celtic nations and discover that Celtic music is very much alive in the present day and at the heart of a new Celtic identity in western Europe.

Who were the Celts?

Defining a 'Celt' is notoriously difficult. There are a number of theories as to who the Celts were, where they came from and how they saw themselves. When we describe something or someone as 'Celtic', are we talking about a culture, an ethnic group or an identity? The simple answer is that there is no definitive answer, though on balance most modern historians are more inclined to see the Celts in terms of a cultural movement rather than a migration of peoples, though this may have been part of the picture.

Before heading off on his journey Dónal met with Dr Éamon Ó Ciosáin from Maynooth University (NUIM) near Dublin, who is an authority on the Celtic languages. According to Dr Ó Ciosáin interest in the Celts grew from the sixteenth century and the first steps in what we would call a scientific approach to the subject came around 1700:

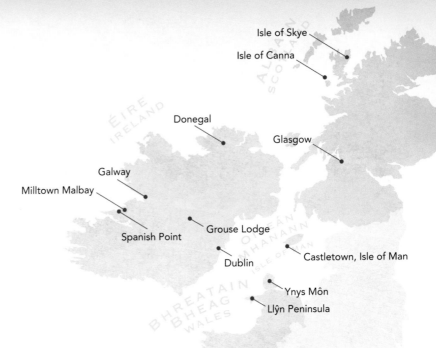

Isle of Skye

Isle of Canna

Donegal

Glasgow

ÉIRE
IRELAND

ALBAIN
SCOTLAND

Galway

Milltown Malbay

Spanish Point

Grouse Lodge

Dublin

Castletown, Isle of Man

Ynys Môn

Llŷn Peninsula

BHREATAIN
BHEAG
WALES

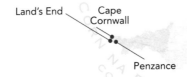

Land's End

Cape
Cornwall

Penzance

CORNWALL

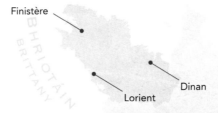

Finistère

BHRIOTÁIN
BRITTANY

Dinan

Lorient

Finisterre

A Coruña

Vigo

Santiago
de Compostela

GAILÍS
GALICIA

ASTÚIRÍS
ASTURIAS

Above: Dr Éamon Ó Ciosáin.
Previous page: Celtic gold torc.

'There were people from a few different countries collecting words and they began to notice the same word in Irish and in Breton were very similar. At that stage it was a sort of a learned enterprise, the uneducated people of Scotland, Ireland and Brittany had no idea that their languages were related.'

What we can be fairly certain of is that Celtic culture has its origins in central Europe nearly 3,000 years ago. The name comes from the Greek 'Keltoi' and was used to describe a variety of peoples in central and western Europe to the north of the classical world. The Romans described the people of

what is now France as 'Gauls' and there are records of them describing themselves as Celts. The Gauls of Gaul are thought to have been a Celtic tribe and variations of the name also appear in Iberia (Galicia) and Turkey (Galatia).

The one unifying feature of all the early Celtic peoples is language and with language comes music. The Celtic languages are a branch of the Indo-European languages and are closely connected with two influential cultures that spread from central Europe – the Hallstatt and the La Tène.

The Hallstatt culture named for its most important archaeological site in Austria was the dominant culture across

Hallstatt, Austria, the village that gives its name to the earliest recognised Celtic culture.

much of Europe from around 800 to 500 BC. It was renowned for its elaborate metal work and had strong trading links with its neighbours to the south. The influence of this early Celtic culture and its language is believed to have spread right across continental Europe from Iberia and Britain in the west as far as central Turkey in the east. The Hallstatt culture was gradually replaced throughout much of Europe by the more sophisticated La Tène culture, its direct successor.

La Tène is named for its most important archaeological site in Switzerland and it is from this era that much of what today defines Celtic culture originates including the 'swirling' style of Celtic design. This was to be the zenith of Celtic cultural influence in Europe.

As Rome continued to expand many of the continental Celts were absorbed into the Roman Empire and their language and culture began to decline. The language fragmented into different branches and the areas of Celtic cultural dominance were pushed more and more to the periphery of the Roman world.

Today in most of continental Europe little is left of this

Poulnabrone Dolmen, Co Clare.

Cornwall and Brittany. What all of these areas have in common is that the languages that have survived are Insular Celtic that is, languages from the British Isles. Northwestern Spain (Galicia and Asturias), while having a strong cultural affinity with the Celtic nations, is not included as the Celtic languages of Iberia died out hundreds of years ago.

As with the origins of the Celts themselves there is no definitive explanation for how the Celtic languages evolved. There are thought to have been several branches of Continental Celtic spoken by the Celts of the European mainland including those in Iberia. The Insular variety developed in Britain and Ireland and to complicate things further there are also two main branches of the surviving Celtic languages, Goidelic (Q-Celtic) in Ireland, Scotland and the Isle of Man and Brythonic (P-Celtic) in Wales, Brittany and Cornwall. How these separate

once great culture except for archaeological sites, Celtic place names and fragments of the language that have been absorbed by those that replaced it. In the west however it was a different matter, far from the centre of imperial power isolated pockets of Celtic culture managed to survive along the Atlantic coasts. Dr Ó Ciosáin added, 'If you look at the way that everybody travelled by sea, traded over the sea in the old days going down the western coasts of Europe and on. If you look at it in historical terms there is no reason why songs and languages shouldn't have travelled up.'

Language
Today the 'Celtic nations' are those areas of western Europe where Celtic language has managed to survive to some degree into the modern era; Scotland, Ireland, the Isle of Man, Wales,

Reproduced by permission of the Librarian, Maynooth University, from the collections of St Patrick's College, Maynooth.

Callanish standing stones on the Isle of Lewis.

The evolution of the Celtic languages continues to be a matter of scholarly debate but one thing we do know is that the Breton language of Brittany originally came from Britain. Following the end of Roman control in Britain in AD 410 Germanic tribes from what is now Germany and Denmark began migrating to Britain. We know them today as the Anglo Saxons and it is they that laid the foundations of the nation of England. The Celtic culture of the Britons, was pushed further west and north by the new arrivals and many even took to the sea and migrated south to Brittany and some as far as northern Spain. The Breton language is closely related to Welsh and Cornish and as we shall discover these areas also retain a strong musical affinity.

but related language groups developed is not clear. Perhaps they are the ancestors of one original Celtic language or perhaps they are the result of different language migrations from the continent. The Q-Celtic/P-Celtic theory holds that the Goidelic languages have a common continental ancestor along with the extinct Celtiberian and Gallaecian languages of Iberia, while the Brythonic languages evolved from another group along with the now extinct Gaulish language.

In more recent years this theory has been challenged by the Insular Celtic hypothesis. This argues that both Brythonic and Goidelic groups evolved from a common Insular ancestor while the Celtic languages of the continent evolved separately. According to Dr Ó Ciosáin, the original Celtic language was spoken in most of northern France and seems to have spread from there to the islands of Great Britain and Ireland.

Celtic crosses at Clonmacnoise.

The Songlines

As the once great Celtic culture of continental Europe came to an end its legacy lived on in the west, in the rugged peninsulas of Wales, Cornwall and Brittany and along the wild Atlantic coasts of Ireland, Scotland and Galicia. These last Celtic refuges had one advantage that enabled the culture to survive; they were all connected by the sea. The ancient trading routes that had been in use along Europe's Atlantic coasts since the Bronze Age were a vital connection between these Celtic outposts. It was these familiar lines of communication that encouraged the Britons to head south to Brittany and Spain. As Dr Éamon Ó Ciosáin explains:

'Looking at the music of the Celtic countries where one can see a definite similarity among both language groups would be in accapella or solo-voice singing. As to whether there would be a connection between the actual language families, that you would have a style of music in say Wales

Megalithic art at Newgrange, County Meath.

Profile – Dónal Lunny

Dónal Lunny is popularly regarded as having been central to the twentieth century renaissance of Irish music. One of nine siblings he was born in Tullamore, County Offaly, but was raised in County Kildare. He collaborated early on with his local friend Christy Moore and since the 1970s Dónal has had involvement with some of the most innovative bands to emerge from Ireland including Planxty, the Bothy Band, Moving Hearts, Coolfin, Mozaik, LAPD, Usher's Island , Zoë Conway and Máirtín O'Connor (ZoDoMo), and most recently with The Atlantic Arc Orchestra, which aspires to combine musicians from some or all of the Celtic nations.

He has toured across the world, collaborating with musicians of many different cultures. Dónal plays guitar, keyboards, bodhrán and is an early exponent of the bouzouki in Irish music.

Dónal co-founded Mulligan Records and produced seventeen albums for the label. Since then he has produced tracks for and collaborated on albums with Kate Bush, Mark Knopfler, Indigo Girls, Clannad, Sinéad O'Connor, Baaba Maal and many others. He produced the internationally acclaimed album for EMI, *Common Ground*, featuring such artists as Bono, Neil and Tim Finn, and Elvis Costello.

He continues his work in studio production, while occasionally composing music for theatre, television and film. He is a member of Aosdána. In 2008 Dónal received an Honorary Doctorate in music from Trinity College and in 2009 was appointed Artist in Residence at the Irish World Academy of Music and Dance at the University of Limerick (UL).

In 2017 Dónal was awarded the TG4 Gradam Ceoil Lifetime Achievement Award for his contribution to Irish music. In their citation the awarding committee said:

'Face any direction in Irish traditional music and you will probably see or hear this multi-talented musician. He has been a consistent presence at the forefront of excellence and change in Irish traditional music for almost fifty years. His music, bands, record label, partnerships, compositions and collaborations combine to map pivotal points on the modern journey of our music. He is a committed and generous artist, curious and open in his adoption of new technologies. He has for many years been an ambassador for Irish traditional music worldwide, and is still travelling.'

Dónal continues to record and perform across the world.

Cornwall's abundant tin, like here at Botallack mine, made it an important trade centre in the Celtic world.

and Brittany which would be different from say Ireland and Scotland, that would be a harder question.

Traditional music in Wales was stamped out by the church so in a way we are not in the best position to be able to say is there a common body of music between Wales and Brittany. In terms of Irish and Scottish music there are clear similarities.

The Bretons of all the Celtic peoples are probably the most aware of their identity, they are very aware of the fact that Welsh is in a strong position and it is very close to Breton. In the old days the 'Onion Johnnies' would head over to Wales from northern Brittany – they would go over on bicycles to sell onions for a season.

So you have human contact, you have the place names, and you have the influence in Brittany of Welsh language media and television. There has also always been a strong awareness in Brittany of Ireland in terms of politics, language and culture. Irish music is extremely popular in Brittany, some Breton musicians would almost prefer to play Irish music than their own.

There is a definite relationship between the revival of the

The specific form that the Bretons have of 'call and respond' which is the dance music in the Breton Fest Noz – the Breton Cèilidh – the best dancers will prefer the human voice because you can get more rhythm inflection and feel into it, that is the feeling anyway that the unaccompanied voice is the best form for dancing. You have to sing these songs at speed so you have to master the language in order to be able to do that so it's an interesting phenomenon where song and music is attracting people towards the language; it gives the language visibility and it gives it a context.

In a similar way people are often attracted to Irish by the lyrics of a song by some well-known group or singer and go on to learn the language. There is a very definite connection between the revival and continuation of the music, the oral traditions of singing and the languages themselves. Apart from anything else musicians travel throughout the world so the languages are now also being heard across the world.'

So along this Atlantic highway people, ideas, language, culture and music continue to flow. Today there are common songs, familiar tunes, instruments and dances that connect these seemingly disparate places. It is in the music of the Celtic Songlines that the most compelling evidence can still be found that those ancient connections have endured.

Cape Cornwall.

music and the oral traditions of singing and the languages themselves. You can see for example how a different population coming from a different place could have ended up with differences in the language if you look at how the Irish language, which was brought over to Scotland evolved through its contact with the Norse – a lot of the pronunciation of Scots Gaelic is different from Irish because of the influence of the Norse.

In all the Celtic countries, particularly in Ireland and in Brittany, the music and song, particularly song, has attracted and is attracting people to the language, to learn the language. People who would know a little bit of the language often become more proficient from learning the songs and often become fluent in the language in that way.

Celtic Language Groupings

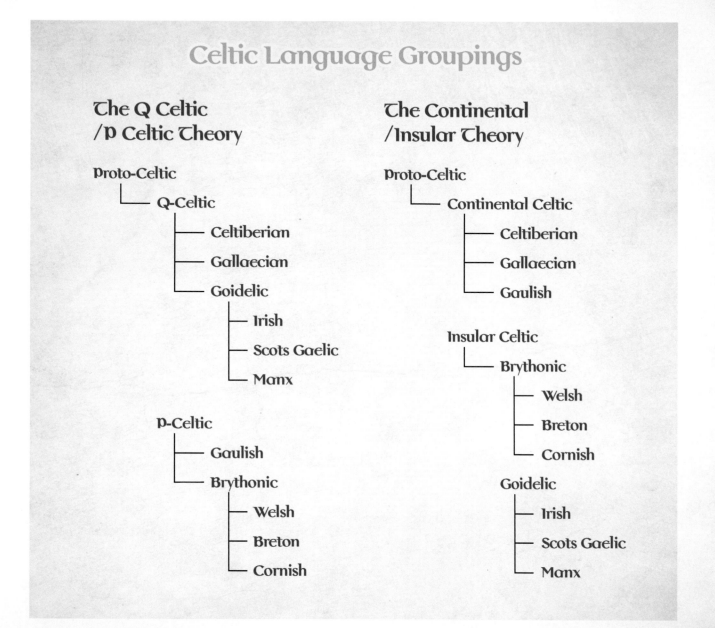

The Q Celtic /P Celtic Theory

Proto-Celtic
└── Q-Celtic
    ├── Celtiberian
    ├── Gallaecian
    └── Goidelic
        ├── Irish
        ├── Scots Gaelic
        └── Manx

P-Celtic
├── Gaulish
└── Brythonic
    ├── Welsh
    ├── Breton
    └── Cornish

The Continental /Insular Theory

Proto-Celtic
└── Continental Celtic
    ├── Celtiberian
    ├── Gallaecian
    └── Gaulish

Insular Celtic
└── Brythonic
    ├── Welsh
    ├── Breton
    └── Cornish

Goidelic
├── Irish
├── Scots Gaelic
└── Manx

Home to Donegal

Our journey begins in County Donegal, Ireland's far northwest. It was here, in the village of Rann na Feirste (Ranafast), that Dónal Lunny spent many a childhood summer and here that he first fell in love with Irish music and the Gaelic language.

This remote part of Donegal is one of the few areas in Ireland where the Irish language has endured as a native tongue and is still widely spoken. It is part of the Donegal Gaeltacht, one of several Gaeltacht areas along Ireland's western coast where Irish is still predominant.

For Dónal growing up in Kildare near Dublin in the east of Ireland, his regular visits to his mother's home place at Ranafast were like a window into a different Ireland that was still very much acquainted with its Celtic past.

Donegal is the picture-postcard Irish landscape from the majestic Mount Errigal to the crashing Atlantic with its battered cliffs and unspoilt beaches. There is an unreal, almost mythical quality to the landscape.

As we will see so often on this journey it is this very isolation that has made it possible for much of the area's heritage to remain. The isolation of the island of Ireland itself enabled Celtic language and culture to survive here relatively intact for hundreds of years.

The process of decline in Celtic culture was slow and piecemeal as the island fell more and more under English influence. The struggle for Irish independence and autonomy is well documented elsewhere but there can be no doubt that the greater the English influence the more marked the decline in Celtic culture.

Much like the Celts of Europe earlier, the Celts of Ireland remained strongest in the Atlantic fringes, in the far western reaches of the country farthest from the seat of English control in Dublin. This western defiance is reflected today in the remaining Gaeltacht areas, where Gaelic culture, language and music remain strongest, being situated along the Atlantic coast in the west of Ireland – the southwestern peninsulas, Connemara, Mayo and Clare in the far west and in Donegal in the northwest.

As well as being strongholds of the language these areas also share a musical independence that is still apparent today. It has often been argued that music itself is a universal language; when it comes to Irish traditional music at least there is a clear affiliation between the traditions of the Gaelic language and the music.

The fragmented landscape in which the language in Ireland survives was historically divided into four key dialectical groups, corresponding roughly to Ireland's four provinces, Munster, Leinster, Connacht and Ulster. Leinster, where the English 'Pale' was located – centred in Dublin – saw its native language effectively become extinct by the late nineteenth century. In the other provinces however the language clung on in the more remote areas and survived into the modern era in small, isolated pockets that would become what we now term as Gaeltacht areas.

What is notable about the tenacious survival of the language in the west is that there is a strong correlation with the strength of traditional music in these areas too. The most

Dónal with Mairéad Ní Mhaonaigh in Rannafast.

influential areas in Irish music broadly correspond to these linguistic outposts though in virtually every case the musical footprint is larger than the linguistic one.

When we talk about regional styles in Irish music we could equally be talking about the dialects of the language. The regional variation is most apparent in fiddle playing; the southwest and the Sliabh Luachra area in particular in Cork and Kerry, the Clare style from County Clare on the west coast and in the northwest the Sligo style and the Donegal style both being highly influential.

In the modern era these regional styles have become less pronounced as musicians from Ireland and further afield share and interact with each other, yet these variations still exist. Being Ireland's most northern county, Donegal has long had historical links with Scotland, both in terms of short-term economic migration and permanent migration, particularly to the city of Glasgow.

This constant to and fro of people has had a marked influence on the traditional music of Donegal that shows strong Scottish influences, and has also brought Irish influence to the music of Scotland. As well as the common jigs and reels found across Ireland, in Donegal the 'Highland' related to the Scottish 'Strathspey' is also very popular. This highland influence in the style has often brought proponents of the Donegal style into conflict with more conservative elements within Irish traditional music.

Dónal's first leg of his journey along the Celtic Songlines is a short and familiar one to Donegal to meet with old friend

Mairéad Ní Mhaonaigh, lead singer of Altan and his brother Manus who now lives in Ranafast where he runs a recording studio. Manus is a member of the Scottish group Capercaillie, one of the pioneers in the modern Celtic music movement. For Mairéad and Manus the interplay between Irish and Scottish music is obvious with many common and related tunes and songs in both repertoires. Strong links in the mythology and folklore of both areas is also apparent attesting to the generations old links between Scotland and Donegal.

For Mairéad it is clear that the music is linked to the language:

'I always felt that it correlates with the type of Celtic language that you speak. Here we speak Gaelic and in Scotland and the Isle of Man they have a commonality. When I hear the music of those three places, especially the songs, they sound very similar and they have similar themes.

You get common stories, especially things to do with the sea, it starts up in Scandinavia and comes down the western coast. You'll find a common song that could be Norwegian or maybe a Viking song, you don't really know where it came from but the common theme is there. It's the same with certain tunes, you've heard the melody of it before, it's kind of related. There is a lot of commonality, and between here and Scotland it is very strong and it has remained strong over the centuries. For example my grandmother had Irish parents but was born in Scotland; they say that forty per cent of Glaswegians have Donegal ancestors! We are very lucky in Ireland to have such a variety of colour in accents and it's the same with the music, and the styles of music are correlated with the language I think.'

Manus Lunny.

Song – 'A Bhean Udaí Thall'

Recorded on Altan's 1989 album *A Horse With a Heart*, 'A Bhean Udaí Thall' is a traditional song, of which many variations are found in Ireland, Scotland and elsewhere. Translated variously as 'The Two Sisters', 'Twa Sisters' or 'The Woman Yonder', it is a classic example of a an Irish narrative ballad and a murder ballad. In Scotland it is sometimes known as 'A Bhean Eudach' or 'The Jealous Woman' or 'The Cruel Sister'. The song tells a story and takes the form of a narrative poem recited by two characters; a drowning woman and a young girl who seeks to usurp her position as a wife and mother. In her dying breaths the drowning wife curses the young girl who seeks to take her place. Variations on this theme can be found in many songs in Ireland and Scotland as well as northern parts of England, the last areas of Celtic influence in that country.

Manus Lunny in his studio in Donegal.

For Manus his involvement with the Scottish group Capercaillie has opened his ears to the possibilities of Celtic music:

'Thirty years ago Celtic music to me went as far the Irish borders but since then I have realised how Celtic music is a huge family of musicians that stretches from the north of Scotland down to the north of Spain. Even before I went to Scotland, my cousins from this area in Ranafast and the Rosses all worked and lived in Scotland at some stage; there was a huge connection between this area and Scotland in fact Glasgow is the capital of Donegal and any Donegal person will tell you that.

It's remarkable if you travel to Brittany, Galicia or Asturias the music is very similar, and the approach is very similar; they have jigs and they have reels, and they play the pipes and they play fiddles and some of the tunes can actually sound the same.'

Profile – Altan

Altan were formed in County Donegal in 1987 by vocalist and fiddler Mairéad Ní Mhaonaigh and her husband, Belfast-born flute and whistle player, Frankie Kennedy. This husband and wife duo gained acclaim and popularity for their performances in folk clubs in Dublin and Belfast in the early 1980s. Gradually the duo grew organically into a band and in the mid 1980s decided on the name Altan taken from a mysterious lake found beside Mount Errigal in Donegal. Ciarán Curran on bouzouki and Mark Kelly on guitar joined Ní Mhaonaigh and Kennedy to form the original lineup and both remain with the band to this day. Fiddler Paul O'Shaughnessy joined not long afterwards giving the band its distinctive two-fiddle sound. When O'Shaughnessy left, Donegal fiddler Ciarán Tourish replaced him. Guitarist Dáithí Sproule joined on guitar followed by accordionist Dermot Byrne. After several years with the band Byrne left and was replaced by accordionist Martin Tourish, completing the band's current line up.

Mairéad Ní Mhaonaigh.

Since their first album *Horse with a Heart* in 1989 the band have released eleven further albums that have consistently met with critical and commercial success. Altan continue to remain true to their Donegal roots and are strong advocates for the Donegal style within traditional music.

Artists they have collaborated with over the years include Dónal Lunny, Steve Cooney, Dolly Parton, Eddi Reader, Mary Chapin Carpenter and many more.

Altan have toured extensively across Europe, North America, Australia and Japan.

In the Beginning

Next we make the short journey south along Ireland's west coast to County Galway, where Dónal met up with Simon O'Dwyer, an expert in the early music of Ireland. According to Simon there are some connections that have been established between the traditional music of modernity and with the music of ancient Ireland. Simon sees the most relevance in this regard in singing and in particular the Sean-nós a cappella traditions from the west of Ireland and in religious ceremonies of some of the Scottish islands that also seem likely to be very old.

There is a description of *crónán*, voice purring or throat singing, used to accompany a song in a ceremony praising Saint Colmcille (Columba), the monk who founded the monastery of Iona in Scotland. According to Simon it also appears that the Bronze Age horns of Ireland and Britain are tuned to play within the human voice range and may have been accompanied by singing:

Demonstrating some of the ancient instruments in Galway.

Simon O'Dwyer.

'We know very little about the music itself, there are no recordings, and as regards instruments there are very few surviving from antiquity but we are lucky in Ireland as we have more than most other places. Generally they tend to be horns and trumpas made of bronze. The oldest known reference is by Giraldus Cambrensis in the thirteenth century. He describes a monk travelling in Wales who had one around his neck and a priest who didn't like that idea but when he tried to play it himself he had a stroke! There are a couple of examples of other instruments including a bassoon-type instrument found in County Mayo and a set of overtone pipes from Wicklow like whistles. You find similar instruments in Scandinavia, but Ireland is the only place where there is a set of them and they happen to be the oldest instruments from Ireland. They are about 4,000-years-old and that's the very beginning of the Bronze Age, the cusp between the end of the Stone Age and the beginning of the Bronze Age.

The eighth-century Enniskillen horns are believed to have been played as a pair accompanying a group of musicians. One of these horns survives and most importantly they are depicted in an illumination from the eighth-century Vespasian Psalter.

There are references to the lyre in the *Táin Bó Fraích* and it is also depicted in the eighth-century Vespasian Psalter. There are an astonishing number and variety of pre-Viking musical instruments in Ireland particularly.

Because they are bronze, they survive; they are robust and they've been turning up right up until very recently and there are now more than 100 in Ireland, that's forty per cent of the world population of metal wind instruments!

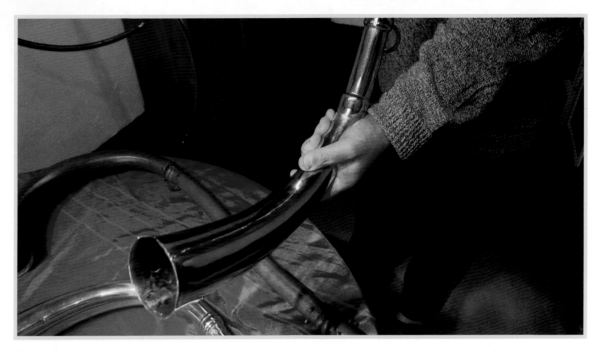

Simon demonstrates an ancient trumpa.

The other instruments that inevitably would have been around at the time, stringed instruments and wind instruments, didn't survive. It is possible that horns were part of an overall spectrum of music and a lot of them, particularly the Bronze Age ones, are tuned in the vocal range so that makes us think maybe they were used to accompany singing.

Many of them are complete and we can reproduce instruments and they work very well together in tune. That implies that there may have been a common tuning in Ireland in the Bronze Age. The tuning is very similar to today, you can play them along with modern music.

We have to look at Ireland and Britain then in a different way than we do now. The Irish Sea acted as a highway connecting rather than dividing the two islands. We know from Iron Age trumpets that the family you find in Ireland once occurred in Wales and there are two examples of instruments that are common to Ireland and Scotland. The triple pipes, which were mouth pipes, you'll find in carvings both in Ireland and in Scotland. Interestingly they had a drone and you had to circular-breathe to play them.'

Simon has had some of the reproduction Bronze Age horns acoustically tested at the University of Edinburgh (UoE) and they have concluded that the end-blown horns were most likely played as single-note instruments, which in effect means you are playing a drone.

'I am very persuaded that this is how they were used, as far back as the Bronze Age and probably earlier, as cattle horns, to the time of stone circles and megalithic buildings 5,000 or 6,000 years ago.

The Bronze-Age horns are clearly derived and ritualised

from cattle horns and that leads forward into the elongated, Iron-Age, sheet-bronze trumpas that are designed to go up in the air and are parade instruments, leading forward to today where you have the pipes.

If you look at a piper as he is carefully tuning up his drones, he takes such time with it and you can hear as he gets them perfect until they are singing together. He, I believe, is perpetrating the ancient, ancient music of Ireland and Britain. It's that ancientness that gives it its power and its popularity, that's why it's popular around the world today I believe.'

Sean-nós Singing

The Sean-nós or the 'old style' of singing was once prevalent throughout Ireland and is believed to be one of the longest surviving musical traditions on the island.

In its simplest form it is a straightforward style of unaccompanied singing, though often it can be quite elaborate in terms melody, tone and rhythm. The songs sung in the Sean-nós style are often long, story-telling songs that are emotionally charged dealing typically with subjects of loss, love and sadness.

As with musical style in Ireland in general, Sean-nós singing follows familiar regional variations with the principle styles being those of the southwest, west and northwest.

Sean-nós singing has been compared to north-African singing and it has been hypothesized that the style reached Ireland via the Atlantic trade routes, though there is little real evidence for this theory.

West to Clare

Milltown Malbay, County Clare, is a place synonymous with Irish music and home to the Willie Clancy Summer School. Musicians from as far away as Argentina and Japan gather here every summer to learn from each other and to exchange ideas.

Dónal has come here to meet his good friend and longtime speaker at the festival, the fiddler Paddy Glackin. Paddy teaches at the summer school and has played throughout the Celtic world, no better man to ask about the connections between Europe's Celtic musical traditions:

'The whole tapestry of the music is what makes it so different, the musician from Donegal will play it very differently than the musician from Kerry or indeed the musician from Clare and vice versa. Donegal music has its own accent but there is no doubt about it that it has close ties with the music of Scotland, particularly in repertoire.

Right up the western seaboard there is a complete continuation of a culture there that we share with Scotland, I mean we are the same people. We have the same language,

Street sign, Milltown Malbay.

In Lynch's pub, Milltown Malbay.

Lynch's pub, Milltown Malbay.

Dónal and Paddy Glackin in Lynch's, Milltown Malbay.

we play roughly the same music and we share the same games, shinty and hurling so there is a huge cultural connection between both countries.

Séamus [Ennis] was one of the most important people in preserving the music. When you think of the huge collection of his that is in the Department of Irish Folklore taken from all over the country, music and song, folklore, everything, he was a phenomenal person. I had the good fortune to get to know him well and spent many's a night with him, so it's extra special to have the fiddle that Séamus used to play on.'

A reminder of the great Séamus Ennis in Lynch's.

Profile – Paddy Glackin

Born in Dublin in 1954, Paddy Glackin is one of Ireland's most accomplished fiddle players. The son of the Scottish-born, Donegal fiddler Tom Glackin, he has been one of the leading exponents of the driving Donegal fiddle style in Irish music.

Paddy pursued classical training in Dublin and plays with his two brothers Kevin and Seamus as The Glackins.

He first became known for playing with Sligo flute player John Egan before rising to prominence as a member of the original lineup of the Bothy Band with Dónal Lunny.

He later forged a long-running partnership with Bothy Band guitarist Mícheál Ó Domhnaill who passed away in 2007. As well as that he became a well-known producer and broadcaster. He was the Irish Arts Council's first Traditional Music Officer.

He has gained acclaim for recordings made with a variety of pipers including Paddy Keenan.

Song – 'The Munster Cloak'

'The Munster Cloak' or 'An Fhalaingín Mhuimhneach', sometimes known as 'The Spanish Cloak' or 'Mantle on Mantle' is a well-known traditional tune that according to some stories was introduced to Ireland by shipwrecked sailors from the Spanish Armada in 1588. Though this tale is unlikely to be true the tune does sometimes draw comparisons with Iberian music in general and may owe something of its structure to influence from that part of Europe.

It does bear a striking resemblance to the Spanish Dance, Danzas Española, Number 6 composed by Enrique Granados in the late nineteenth century.

There are various documented versions of 'The Munster Cloak' and similar tunes going back to the eighteenth century, but probably the best-known version today is that recorded by The Chieftains in 1964, following which it became fairly common in the Irish traditional repertoire.

The cloak of the title is the traditional black, hooded cloak commonly worn by women in County Cork up until the first half of the twentieth century.

Willie Clancy Summer School

The Willie Clancy Summer School (*Scoil Samhraidh* Willie Clancy) is the original and biggest of the annual musical summer schools held every summer in Ireland. It was first held in Milltown Malbay on the County Clare coast back in 1973 and is named in memory of the famous local uilleann piper Willie Clancy who came from the town and died that year. The school attracts hundreds of students from across the world. The town transforms for a week-long music festival. As well as lessons, lectures and courses the town hosts numerous concerts, sessions, gigs and dances right throughout the week.

Every year the school is opened with the Breandán Breathnach Memorial Lecture with lessons given each day by leading musicians in the uilleann pipes, flute, harp, banjo, tin whistle, concertina, fiddle, accordion, harmonica and set dancing.

Spanish Point

At Spanish Point just down the road from Milltown (and up and down Ireland's west coast) the Spanish Armada, sent to invade England by King Philip of Spain in 1588, foundered in stormy seas with the loss of twenty-four ships. Up to 5,000 men are thought to have lost their lives and the events of the Armada are recorded in local legend and music.

We will never know how many of those men carried the music of Galicia and Asturias with them but the famous Irish tune 'The Munster Cloak' is said to gave been developed from music brought a-shore by Iberian sailors who survived the wreckage of the Spanish Armada here in County Clare.

Dónal and Paddy play 'The Munster Cloak' at Spanish Point, County Clare.

The Collectors

We have come to Dublin and to the Irish Traditional Music Archive on Merrion Square. This wonderful multi-media resource is open to the general public and contains a wealth of information on Irish music down through the ages.

If anyone can give us an insight into the evolution of Irish music it is archive director, Grace Toland, an accomplished singer herself. Dónal accompanies Grace in a beautiful rendition of the evocative 'The Four Marys', a song that exemplifies for Grace the close connections between the Irish and Scottish traditions. 'I think it's one of those songs that shows how interconnected Ireland is with all sorts of countries but especially with Scotland. It's shown all through the collections of the Irish Traditional Music Archive and locally with singers and musicians but then you also see it in the printed and manuscript works we have here and in the recordings that we have.'

Grace comes from the Inishowen Peninsula in the far north of County Donegal, an area with strong cultural ties to

The Irish Traditional Music Archive in Dublin.

Dónal with Grace Toland at the Irish Traditional Music Archive in Dublin.

Scotland and the version of 'The Four Marys' she sings was taught to her by a man who spent his life travelling in Scotland and England and all over Europe, bringing songs back into the tradition.

For Grace the relative isolation of Ireland is what has enabled the tradition of music here to survive:

'Isolation is a factor because any community that doesn't have that regular traffic in and out, and we are talking pre-recording, at a time when music would have been bounded by how far you could travel.

Now some people might only travel one mile away from their community, other people could have travelled 1,000 miles. In those situations you will always see the traditional and sometimes the conservatism within it allows it to have stayed almost pure up to a point.

Our connections are by the sea, we are right out on the edge and in saying that, when you see Irish musicians and singers they've brought something back in to the tradition, and they were well able to mould it.'

Recording and documenting that tradition has been vital to its survival and in particular the advent of recording technologies just at the time when the very survival of the tradition was under most threat in the early part of the twentieth century.

'The recording of music on 78s, especially in America, it saved music in a time that in Ireland that sort of recording industry wasn't here. You had a community with access to state-of-the-art technology, they caught fantastic musicians as you see in Francis O'Neill's collection. The same could be said of the Irish in London in the 1950s and 1960s, the music recorded there by the likes of Reg Hall. There was better music being played in London in that time because of the mass emigration.'

Emigration though devastating for Ireland may ironically have played a role in preserving Irish music for future generations.

'The effect of emigration was devastating on the country but in musical terms it actually helped get the music into print and recorded, and also that whole movement of meeting new cultures, clashing and joining, brought all sorts of new influences back into the country.'

Director Emeritus at the archive is Nicholas Carolan, who has spent years researching and cataloging the work of music collectors and musicologists like Breandán Breathnach and Séamus Ennis, but just how vital has their work been to the continuation of the tradition?

Nicholas believes that the Irish tradition has been handed down in a very natural way from generation to generation:

'Somebody makes up a tune or a song, plays it, sings it, people like it, learn it and pass it on. In older times there was only an oral tradition before music was written down, you're talking about a period of about 10,000 years of human habitation in Ireland and music has only been notated for about 400 of those in this country.

Up to the seventeeth century, a really destructive century when Gaelic civilisation almost came to an end, there was a system of patronage of poets and of professional musicians. They created a whole body of music that wouldn't have been created by people who were working at a folk level, working with their hands.'

Grace Toland at work at the Irish Traditional Music Archive in Dublin.

When we see Irish music played today it is easy to forget the debt it owes to the bardic tradition in Gaelic culture. Bardic poets were once common in Ireland and Scotland, trained in bardic schools they travelled across the Gaelic lands and published widely.

'For many hundreds of years Ireland and Scotland were simply the same cultural region in terms of language, cultural life and attitude to life generally. You had Scottish pipers coming to Ireland to be trained and Irish harpers going across for patronage to Gaelic Scotland. Most of the reels we play are Irish reels, but the form, the actual number of bars for example is a tune type that has come in from Scotland, so there is an intimate connection. We still have in the body of Irish traditional music a great deal of material created during the bardic period and of course it has changed and morphed and evolved since. Traditional music as we know it nowadays is relatively modern, developed in the last 300–400 years. If there were earlier connections they were thousands of years ago or even tens of thousands of years ago.

Obviously thousands of years ago different languages came into Ireland, from the continent, from Spain, from France, from Britain. Megalithic builders came here and people introduced farming here, all of these cultural innovations came with language but they also came with music.

Traditional music is a very complex body of material; there are different layers of time, layers of place and layers of personality. When it comes down to the essentials it's the oral character of it, the fact that it was passed on essentially from person to person and then eventually from generation to generation.

Traditional dance tunes are short, maybe twenty or thirty seconds and then repeated, songs are structured in verses, and this is all related to memory and the passing it on in an oral tradition. That's the essence of traditional music I think, that it is an oral form of music.'

What of the harp, the symbol of Ireland and once central to Irish music and the bardic culture of Ireland and Scotland?

'The harp has been central to Irish music for about 1,000 years now, it was the classical instrument of Irish music for about 700 of those years and then it started to go into decline and it died in a sense in the nineteenth century for various social reasons. It was partly for musical reasons as well because it's a quiet instrument, it's big and heavy and hard to carry and hard to tune, and it couldn't really compete for ordinary household dancing with the accordion for example.

It began to revive, it came back from the dead really, in the period of the Gaelic League in the 1890s and it has continued since so that the new tradition of the harp is over a 100-years-old now. So it's a strong tradition, there is a whole world of harping now and I think you will hear much more about Irish harping in the future.'

But none of this heritage would have survived without the work of the music collectors of the late nineteenth and early twentieth centuries both in Ireland and within the Irish diaspora.

RTÉ archivist Ian Lee.

'The work of collectors and musicologists has been very important in the history of Irish traditional music. They fall into two groups, those who collected on paper and, in our own time, those who collected on tape, audiotape or video-tape.

The importance was that they preserved tunes, words and songs that would otherwise have vanished. So people like James Goodman, Edward Bunting, Francis O'Neill operated in that kind of world. Tape recording, film and video recording are actually more satisfactory in a way because they capture elements of style that can't be captured on paper.'

Ireland's largest audio-visual archive is held by RTÉ, the national broadcaster and there is an extensive collection of material relating to Irish traditional music.

This year (2017) marks the 70th anniversary of the first field recordings made by the state broadcaster as part of its effort to preserve Ireland's musical heritage.

According to archivist Ian Lee the collection is an invaluable resource that has helped preserve the Irish tradition and enabled it to flourish:

Song – 'Mo Ghile Mear'

Renowned Munster poet Seán Clárach mac Domhnaill wrote the song 'Mo Ghile Mear', 'My Bright Darling' or 'My Gallant Darling' some time in the late eighteenth century in honour of Charles Edward Stuart better known today as Bonnie Prince Charlie. Charles was a claimant to the thrones of Ireland, Scotland, England and France and led the failed Jacobite uprising of 1745 that was finally defeated at the Battle of Culloden in 1746; the last battle on Scottish soil it effectively ended the Jacobite claim to the crown.

Mac Domhnaill, a native of north Cork, was one of the Maigue Poets of County Limerick and the Chief Poet of Munster. 'Mo Ghile Mear' is his best-known poem and is a lament for the lost Jacobite cause and the Stuart claim to the crown. The defeat of Bonnie Prince Charlie was a crushing blow to Gaelic culture in both Scotland and Ireland.

The poem would have been commonly sung and takes the form of the Gaelic goddess Éire (Ireland) lamenting the loss of her 'Gallant Darling':

> He is my champion, my Gallant Darling,
> He is my Caesar, my Gallant Darling,
> I've found neither rest nor fortune
> Since my Gallant Darling went far away.

'Back in 1947 when Radio Éireann went out into the field in those years they were recording on acetate discs, which today are kind of scratchy, tape was much better quality, but

Profile – Séamus Ennis

A leader in the revival of the uilleann pipes, a gifted musician, singer and tin-whistle player, Ennis was also one of the most important song collectors in Irish traditional music, as well as a broadcaster and translator.

Born in Finglas, County Dublin in 1919, his father James Ennis was a piper and dancer and he grew up in a household steeped in Gaelic culture and made regular visits to the Connemara Gaeltacht in County Galway.

One of his first jobs was working for another piper Colm Ó Lochlainn who collected and published Irish ballads and tunes. Here he learnt musical notation that was to prove vital to his later work.

He later worked for the Irish Folklore Commission collecting tunes in Ireland and Scotland and was employed by Brian George of the BBC during their extensive music collecting tour of Ireland and Britain. Ennis was reputedly so proficient in Irish that he could switch with ease between the various regional dialects of the language depending on what part of the country he was in at the time and had no trouble conversing in Scottish Gaelic on his trips to the Highlands and Islands.

Working for Radio Éireann he brought Ireland's traditional music to a wide audience for the first time. He also worked with the legendary American music collector Alan Lomax. As the folk revival took hold in the 1960s he remained a central figure, playing and mentoring up-and-coming musicians, including Liam O'Flynn.

Ian Lee at the RTÉ archive.

the great thing about the acetate discs was that you couldn't record over them. When tape came in it could be used and reused again.

Radio Éireann and later RTÉ and all broadcasting organisations did that, because tape was very expensive and people had to come in under budget. When Ciarán mac Mathúna came along in 1954 or 1955 as a full-time collector generally speaking everything he recorded, and he only recorded on tape, was kept so we got lucky that way and we got lucky with the acetate discs in that several thousand were recorded and they were all kept because they couldn't be used again. As we speak they are being digitised and catalogued and the sound quality will be enhanced, so there are gems awaiting us down the road.'

It was not only Radio Éireann who were collecting at this time however, the BBC also played a major role in recording and preserving many of the old tunes. In fact the BBC beat Radio Éireann to it in the field of collecting in Ireland, because in August 1947 Brian George who was a Donegal man working for the BBC saw that it was very important to go out and collect in Ireland, Scotland, England and Wales.

'He came to Ireland and he employed Séamus Ennis and the two of them went literally around the whole country, Gaeltacht areas and all in August 1947. In that collection they recorded about 300 discs and they still exist. Radio Éireann didn't get going until November 1947 and their first port of call was Peig Sayers in Dún Chaoin, but before they recorded Peig they recorded some Spanish sailors who were marooned on Valentia Island and they sang fantastically!'

For the first time we were getting close to the authentic sound of Irish traditional music.

'Before that, if you wanted Dónal Lunny to come in and play music you had to bring him into the studio and he might be uncomfortable with the formal atmosphere of a studio. Now people were being recorded in their own houses, recorded in pubs; they were much more at their ease and very importantly the recordings were brought back and used on air. They weren't secreted away into an archive as such.'

Ian believes that the original intention with these archives was for the recordings to be catalogued and studied by learned and worthy men who would come in and compare versions and analyse their cultural significance.

'I think it came as a surprise to both the BBC and Radio Éireann that this stuff went down very well on air, it worked as an entertainment and as an information medium.'

Much of the bardic tradition has also been preserved through the recordings in the archive, but as Ian noted, the poems and songs have transformed over time.

'If you take the great love songs, and it's reckoned that

The RTÉ Radio Centre.

An old wax cylinder player.

Song – 'The Four Marys'

'The Four Marys' or 'Mary Hamilton' is a traditional Scottish ballad that has enjoyed great popularity in the Irish and Scottish repertoires with its origins possibly going back as far as the sixteenth century.

A version sung by the American folk singer Joan Baez popularised the song in the 1960s, where it became a staple of the folk revival on both sides of the Atlantic.

There are several variants of the song that can be quite different lyrically and can also use different settings but the song always concerns the travails of a lady in waiting to Mary Queen of Scots named Mary Hamilton.

The narrative, probably fictitious, notes how Mary Hamilton becomes pregnant by the King and drowns her baby but is caught in the act and she laments the circumstances that have led to her predicament. The four Marys of the title were the ladies in waiting who attended Mary Queen of Scots from a young age.

An alternate history for the song proposes that it may originate from a similar story relating to a lady in waiting to Catherine, consort of Peter the Great in Russia, from the eighteenth century.

about sixty per cent of the Sean-nós repertoire comprises love songs, songs of unrequited love. Happy love situations didn't appear to inspire poems but unrequited love did! The people who wrote down the words of the great love songs were educated poets; people in their everyday speech would not have used the kind of language that they employed. If you were to compare that for example with the 'Blues' in America, you are dealing with exactly the same themes but the Blues were written in the speech of the ordinary people.

When it comes to Scotland, you can say that the repertoire is almost 100 per cent similar except for the fact that the Scots have their fantastic *Òrain Luaidh* or Waulking songs. Work songs seemed to die out in Ireland, also in Scotland they had a choral tradition up in Lewis where they sang the psalms, which are almost a mirror image of the gospels, they were being sung in the southern United States, they were composed and sung for the same reason. There was very little choral tradition in Ireland apart from the Kilmore Carols that were sung in Kilmore Quay, County Wexford coming up to Christmas.'

RTÉ producer Jim Lockhart is perhaps better know as a member of Celtic rock group Horslips. As a musician who has straddled the traditional and contemporary worlds he believes that the transformation in Irish music over the last fifty years or so has been extraordinary.

'Celtic Rock really was a term that arose after the fact, what we were trying to do basically was just play some music that meant something to us, that had some kind of reference to our own experience and what we had grown up with but that also spoke to who we were.

We have an extraordinary heritage of music in Ireland, a parallel live culture that managed to exist in pretty inauspicious circumstances for an awful long time. That has a lot to do with the sense of responsibility that people feel who inherit the tradition through their family or through their locality. They see it as incumbent on them to preserve the pure drop and it's really important that that has happened down through the years.'

The work of Seán Ó Riada in the 1950s and 1960s has been vital in the survival and later renaissance of Irish music.

'Without Seán Ó Riada none of what has happened in traditional music, since then over the last fifty years would have been possible or even conceivable. He substituted harpsichord for piano, bodhrán for drums and accordion for piano accordion. He changed the whole sound of what ensemble playing of Irish music was. It now underpins a sense of self confidence and a self of identity that we have because it has developed its own legs.'

In the 1970s following the work of Ó Riada, a greater awareness of the wider Celtic cultural world also began to emerge in Ireland, in Britain and on the continent.

'I think from the time that we started hearing Alan Stivell in the early 1970s, we realised that there was a whole Breton dimension to the music we were familiar with, it was related but different. We were always kind of aware of Scottish music, but we didn't know anything about Welsh music, and we didn't even know that Galicia existed by and large.

The fact they we are now aware of this music, principally through the Festival Interceltique de Lorient, we now have this extended fraternity of Celts, it has caused an awareness

Jim Lockhart.

that we are part of a larger family.

The difference that has come about in the popularity of Irish music compared to what it was in the late 1950s is really beyond comprehension. It was a sort of colonial situation in that if it was ours it was to be looked down on; it was only valid if it was presented in the context of a leader in a tux on a concert platform with a piano in a John McCormack type presentation. To have it presented as raw Sean-nós, I remember hearing it described as 'the tune the old cow died of, why would you be listening to that?''

Profile – Francis O'Neill

Francis O'Neill, a native of Bantry, County Cork, born in 1848, was among the multitudes of Irish who left their native land to escape the ravages of the Great Famine. He grew up in a musical household in west Cork and was reputedly an accomplished musician himself playing the pipes, the flute and the fiddle.

He became a sailor and travelled the world and was reportedly shipwrecked in the Pacific and almost starved to death before being rescued. Eventually he reached the United States and settled in Chicago, where he joined the police force in 1873. Despite being shot on duty he steadily rose up the ranks becoming General Superintendent of Police in the city in 1901.

Popularly known from then on as Chief O'Neill he never lost his love of Irish music and in his spare time began collecting and recording the tunes and songs of his native land among the Irish multitudes in America.

O'Neill realised that with a population of more than ten per cent Irish Immigrants from all over the island, the Chicago of that time presented a precious opportunity to record and preserve a musical heritage that was in severe danger of being lost forever. O'Neill set to work with his Scottish friend James O'Neill; as Francis was not able to write music but had an exceptional ear the two worked as a team.

He published several collections in the early twentieth century collating thousands of Irish and Scottish tunes and in 1931 he donated his entire collection to the University of Notre Dame (UND). His role was of major significance to the survival of the Irish tradition with Nicholas Carolan aptly summing up his contribution with the title of his 1997 book on O'Neill, *A Harvest Saved: Francis O'Neill* and *Irish Music in Chicago*.

Profile – Seán Ó Riada

Regarded by many as the most important Irish composer of the twentieth century, Seán Ó Riada played a critical role in forming what today would be recognised as traditional Irish music through the groundbreaking group Ceoltóirí Chualainn.

Born in Cork in 1931 his parents were both musical, his father a Garda originally from County Clare and his mother from the Múscraí Gaeltacht in west Cork. He developed a strong interest in both music and Irish culture from an early age and studied his passions throughout his schooling in Adare, County Limerick and Cork before graduating from University College Cork (UCC), where he read Arts and Music.

He began working in Radio Éireann where he was appointed Assistant Director of Music in 1953. He continued working in radio and also became Music Director of the Abbey Theatre in Dublin and began composing music himself.

His score for the 1959 documentary *Mise Éire* is probably his best-known classical piece, strongly influenced as it is by Irish traditional music. The success of *Mise Éire* led him to further explore Ireland's native folk music in radio programmes and also in researching the tunes, songs and instruments of the musical culture.

This led to the formation of Ceoltóirí Chualainn, probably the most influential group in the history of modern Irish traditional music. Ó Riada dramatically changed the arrangements and instrumentation of what was considered the 'traditional' band introducing the bodhrán, button accordion and removing the drums among many other innovations.

He later settled in the Múscraí Gaeltacht himself and became a lecturer in music at UCC, continuing to compose in traditional, classical and liturgical forms.

Grouse Lodge

Among those joining him for what turns out to be an amazing session are Cormac de Barra, Graham Henderson, John McSherry, Máirtín O'Connor, Éamonn de Barra and Zoë Conway.

The talented young fiddle player, singer and composer Zoë Conway records a stunning tune that comes originally from the Isle of Man, 'The song I'm singing is called 'Uiseag Bheag Ruaidh' which means 'Little Red Bird', I learned it from Gráinne Holland and it's her version of an Isle of Man song and it also has versions in Scotland. It's a lullaby with a really simple melody that is repetitive and very beautiful.'

Dónal arrives at Grouse Lodge Studios, County Westmeath.

Before we leave Ireland and embark on the next stage of our journey to Scotland, Dónal is heading to the Grouse Lodge recording studios in County Westmeath to meet up with some old friends and share what he has discovered so far.

As part of the Celtic Songlines project Dónal will record with the various artists he meets along the way adding layers and complexity to the tracks as he progresses.

He started the process at Manus Lunny's studio in Donegal with Mairéad Ní Mhaonaigh and now at Grouse Lodge he joins several friends to really start laying down the soundtrack of the journey.

Dónal in session at Grouse Lodge Studios.

Dónal is greeted by *(from left)* Graham Henderson, Máirtín O'Connor and Éamonn de Barra at Grouse Lodge Studios.

The legendary accordionist Máirtín O'Connor and piper John McSherry also join Dónal. They both feel that there are clear relationships between the various Celtic styles and traditions.

'Listening to any particular piece of music from another region,' said Máirtín, 'it's amazing what it can suggest for our own music, if we are looking for compatible tunes'. John added, 'I play a lot of tunes from Asturias and Galicia, Breton tunes as well, it just kind of fits in with what we are doing ourselves'.

Flautist Éamonn de Barra believes the music of the various Celtic nations share a basic commonality but they really have their own characteristics too:

'When you find that commonality it allows you to merge the music together and that can be quite an exciting thing. We play an old Welsh tune for example in which you can

Recording at Grouse Lodge.

clearly hear the Breton call and respond structure, but it also hints at an Irish reel. They have a commonality, there is clearly a history there that is connected, sometimes you hear it the reels and in the slower pieces.'

When it comes to defining what is traditional and what is not Éamonn believes the constantly changing nature of the music makes this an almost impossible task.

'People often ask what Irish traditional music is, it's a big question that has been debated for many years and it has never really been resolved and I don't think it ever will because it is ever-changing.

When you are talking about tradition, it is something that is constantly moving and that's the whole beauty of it. It's

Cormac de Barra in session at Grouse Lodge.

Left: Cormac de Barra, *Right:* Graham Henderson.

Zoë Conway in session at Grouse Lodge.

Éamonn de Barra at Grouse Lodge.

Left: Máirtín O'Connor, *Right:* John McSherry.

Éamonn de Barra at Grouse Lodge.

history if it stays exactly the same, and even then it is contested. In the 1970s people listened to what Dónal was doing and they didn't call it traditional music, now it is traditional music but new things that people are doing now are not called traditional music so it's really an ever-evolving thing.'

The awakening of a wider Celtic tradition he believes has been a positive for all of the musicians involved over the last few decades.

'Celtic music has really sprung up over the last forty years or so during which the study of the music and the commonality of the Celtic thread is only something that is quite recent. When musicians started travelling over to Brittany and meeting people like Alan Stivell they began to exchange ideas, Breton music and Irish music, they would be learning from each other.

Celtic music then became a twentieth century phenomenon and it is something that is now in every part of the world. I think the phenomenon of Celtic music and that common thread

Song – 'Ushag Veg Ruy'

'Ushag Veg Ruy' (Manx), 'Uiseag Bheag Ruaidh' (Irish), 'Uiseag Bheag Dhear' (Scottish), or 'Little Red Bird' is a traditional lullaby that originated in the Isle of Man though may ultimately have Scottish roots. Well-known versions are sung by the Manx singer Emma Christian and the Belfast singer Gráinne Holland. A simple, yet beautiful repetitive lullaby, it is probably one of the best-known Manx tunes of this type.

It appears in a collection of Manx ballads and folksongs collected by Arthur William Moore in the late nineteenth century.

From left: Graham Henderson, Máirtín O'Connor and John McSherry at Grouse Lodge.

has brought people together and given them opportunities to express their ideas in a way that wasn't available before.' The sense of community, collaboration and experimentation can only increase in the future he believes.

'This kind of experiment that is happening in this project, I feel that this is exactly what needs to happen to demonstrate the power of bringing similar music together and also to explore things that wouldn't necessarily have been explored before.

What it means for the future is that certain elements will be discovered in Dónal's journey that will open up other possibilities between musicians, it also shows the influence that an individual can have, as Dónal has always been central to that push for change throughout his career.'

Dónal among the beautiful surroundings of Grouse Lodge, County Westmeath.

Profile – Zoë Conway

One of the fastest rising stars of the Irish music scene in recent years is Zoë Conway. Her relaxed yet precise fiddle style and beautiful singing voice have brought her international attention. Playing in a duo with her guitarist husband John McIntyre the pair have gained a reputation as one of the best contemporary folk acts around. She also tours as part of a trad 'supergroup' with Máirtín O'Connor and Dónal Lunny. She has performed with a host of contemporary and traditional stars including Damien Rice, Lisa Hannigan, Nick Cave and Lou Reed.

Zoë Conway in the studio at Grouse Lodge.

Zoë Conway.

Celtic Connections

We are travelling the Celtic superhighway once again, this time north to Scotland, following those same Atlantic currents that brought Celtic culture to these shores in the distant past.

And like those ancient travellers we are bringing music with us, from Ireland Dónal has the core tunes that will help him piece together that common Celtic musical heritage.

Now its time to see how that musical culture has flourished and evolved here in Celtic Europe's northern outpost and to make the first connections in the Celtic Songlines that stretch more than 1,000 miles from Skye to Galicia. This stunning landscape is rich in Celtic history and mythology, it was along Scotland's west coast that travellers from Ireland established the great Celtic Kingdom of Dál Riata. It was here that Saint Columba founded his famous monastery at Iona and it was those Irish, the Scoti, who would eventually lend their name to the great Celtic nation of Scotland. With the native Picts they created a true Celtic culture that stretched from the Hebrides to the Borders, a land rich in poetry, art and song.

Everywhere you look there are reminders of the shared heritage of Ireland and Scotland, in the landscape, in the people and most of all, in the music.

Dónal in Glasgow.

Glasgow.

We have come to Glasgow, Scotland's largest city and a bustling crossroads of Celtic culture.

Here the Royal Conservatoire of Scotland (RCS) runs one of the UK's leading degree courses dedicated to traditional and folk music, where students explore Scotland's unique and dynamic musical traditions. The Conservatoire has a strong relationship with Glasgow's Celtic Connections festival, held in the city every January. Established in 1994 the festival has grown to become one of the biggest celebrations of Celtic music anywhere in the world attracting hundreds of musicians and an audience of more than 100,000.

Donald Shaw is a founder and member of Capercaillie, one of the pioneering bands of Scotland's folk revival in the 1980s and has been the artistic director of Celtic Connections since 2007:

'I'm from Argyll which is right on the west coast and when I was learning Gaelic at school I was always confused about the fact that Argyll translates as 'the Gaels of the east' Earra-Ghàidheal, but I was living in the west. I plucked up the courage one day to ask my Gaelic teacher why this didn't make sense and he said it's because it is named by 'that lot over in Donegal' and they were looking east.'

For Donald, steeped in the tradition of Scotland's west coast, the connections with Ireland are very apparent.

'I notice it most with the music of Donegal, the songs of Donegal and the Gaelic songs of the west coast of Scotland, not only melodically but in the ideas, lyrically as well, in the stories that they are telling. We used to argue that Scotland had all the great songs and Ireland had all the great tunes, but now I'm, not so sure, I think it's a fifty-fifty mix.'

As far as reaching out beyond Scotland and Ireland, the Celtic Connections festival has certainly made musicians aware of that wider Celtic family.

'It took me a while to understand why musically there was such a strong link with regions like Galicia and Asturias, why

Donald Shaw.

you would stumble across tunes that were almost identical. It's all in the fact that the Celts, as a tribe, as a people, they had the oral tradition being the most important part of their culture. So as they travelled through the regions, through Brittany, the north of Spain, Ireland and Scotland, that intensity of the culture always existed within that Celtic bubble if you

Donald and Dónal in younger days!

Donald Shaw and Dónal.

like. Music developed as they travelled, it never dissipated.'

A talented accordion player, Donald was a founder member of Capercaillie, one of the first bands to be labelled as Celtic, who have enjoyed great success since the early 1980s.

'Capercaillie was about trying to explore the possibility of Gaelic song. As a band we were obviously very fortunate to have a singer [Karen Matheson] with a very emotive voice and a very emotive repertoire of songs that she had learned from her grandmother in the Hebrides.

At the time that Capercaillie started to really look at ideas and record in the 1980s. By then a lot of the exploratory work had been done by great musicians like Dónal in Ireland. So we had a starting point to look to and I think we felt we should try and explore where Gaelic song could go.'

And in the tradition of the Scottish Waulking songs of the west coast Donald believes those connections may reach even further afield.

'Those work songs from the Hebrides, Waulking songs, with very tribal rhythms, very poly-rythmic, were kind of almost peculiar to just the west coast of Scotland in Europe, nowhere else in Europe has something like that. It's almost as if you have to go to regions of Africa to find the same kind of style in the songs.'

Being closely involved with the Celtic Connections festival in Glasgow for many years Donald has seen first hand the positive impact it has had and how the fortunes of traditional music in Scotland have transformed over that time.

'Celtic Connections is a really interesting story because it's twenty-five years now since the festival began and it has really been running in parallel with an extraordinary renaissance in traditional and folk music in Scotland. There was a lot of emphasis on creating workshops and festivals for young people, for kids, to get into music and really that has been the backbone of this kind of explosion of how the music has found, more than anything, confidence in what Scottish music

musician with one of the most successful trad bands to come out the Isle of Man, Barrule, having previously studied at the University of the Highlands and Islands (UHI).

Dónal met with them at the Conservatoire to play a couple of reels where Tom explained why Glasgow has become such a magnate for Manx musicians:

'The connections are many and varied, culturally we are connected hugely with the stories from the Isle of Man, Ireland and Scotland and the language really sits in the middle. The Isle of Man in a lot ways reflects its geographical position pretty well, in between the other Celtic nations.'

And the vibrant musical scene in Glasgow in particular seems to appeal to younger Manx musicians.

'Here we are lucky to have a great scene of music, lots of great bands, lots of great sessions, every night of the week, sometimes four or five sessions, there's a really healthy music scene which draws a lot of people up here; then of course we've got this building we are in now, the RCS. '

and traditional music is about.

When I went to school I would have smuggled the accordion into school! I wouldn't really have wanted anyone to see me carrying an instrument like that; there could have been a chance of a beating up on the way out!

Now you could stand at the gates of any rural school in Scotland and if they didn't walk in with a fiddle or a *clàrsach* or a set of pipes it would be unusual. A lot of those musicians are on the main stage themselves now, in bands playing around the festivals. The emphasis is much more on the word connections than the word Celtic. This city is extraordinary for its appetite and opinion about music across the board, if you bring great music to Glasgow, people will come out and see it.'

In Glasgow you will find musicians from right across the Celtic world like brother and sister Tom and Isla Callister from the Isle of Man. Isla is a talented fiddle and concertina player as well as a Manx speaker studying traditional music at the Conservatoire in Glasgow. Tom is now a professional

Dónal arrives at the Celtic Connections office in Glasgow.

Profile – Capercaillie

Formed by accordionist Donald Shaw and vocalist Karen Matheson, Capercaillie is one of the most influential Scottish folk bands of the past thirty years.

Named for the Western Capercaillie, a common wild bird in Donald Shaw's native Argyll they released their first album *Cascade* in 1984. Performing traditional Gaelic songs and tunes as well as English and contemporary songs and making use of a wide range of instruments the band quickly drew a loyal and significant following and were among the first major groups to be described as Celtic.

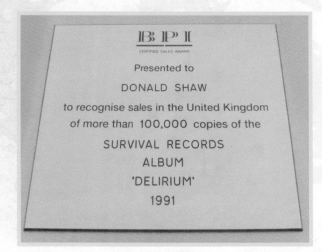

They have enjoyed continued success throughout their career and are still performing today featuring Dónal Lunny's brother Manus on bouzouki and guitar as well as Michael McGoldrick on flute and pipes and Charlie McKerron on fiddle.

Dónal playing with Isle of Man musicians Tom and Isla Callister at The Royal Conservatoire of Scotland.

Canna House

We are on the seas again, this time heading to the island of Canna, the westernmost of the Small Isles in the Inner Hebrides. This area was once part of the Gaelic kingdom of Dál Riata and has retained a strong Celtic culture in its music and language.

The folklorist and historian John Lorne Campbell and his wife Margaret Fay Shaw owned the island and lived at Canna House for more than fifty years. During that time they assembled a remarkable archive of Hebridean culture recording the poetry, songs and music of the area and beyond.

The National Trust for Scotland manage the collection today and Fiona Mackenzie, a Gaelic singer herself, is the archivist charged with curating this incredible collection of material. 'If you look at a map of Scotland, normally we look at it from north to south, but if you turn Scotland on its side you see how Canna is right in the middle of all the trade routes, all the cultural routes between Ireland and Scotland,' said Fiona.

The house is home to an amazing collection of music, folklore and memorabilia from across the Hebrides. The Irish collector Séamus Ennis was among those who collaborated with John Lorne Campbell. 'I think they are still here in spirit if not in body,' said Fiona, 'this house became a great house of music and song.'

Following the Songlines to the Isle of Canna.

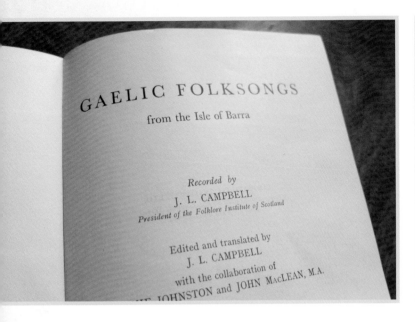

Dónal with Fiona Mackenzie at Canna House.

What is remarkable about Canna House, as well as the incredible collection it holds, is that it has changed very little since John and Margaret were living here.

Fiona is very conscious of her role in continuing the work that started:

'Part of my work is to bring these songs and bring their work back to the foreground of folklore, music and song. They collected over 1,500 recordings made in the Hebrides in the 1930s and 1940s. Margaret transcribed several hundred of the songs in a way that had never been done before and John did immense research into the songs and he formed great relationships too with his singers.

Being a trained classical musician she was able to transcribe songs physically in a way that had never been done in the Hebrides before.

He had the mechanical recording ability when it came to

Canna House.

physically recording the songs but she had the musical ability so together they made a great partnership.'

Margaret's study is still much as it was when she was working at Canna House.

'It's a lovely room and you can almost feel Margaret sitting here at her typewriter.'

Another treasure at Canna House is the typewriter used by Compton Mackenzie to write his 1947 novel *Whisky Galore* that he adapted into a hit movie in 1949. Mackenzie was an ardent Scottish nationalist and a founder of the Scottish National Party.

The book is based on a true story, as Fiona explained, 'The ship, the SS Politician that inspired the story, it went down just off South Uist and Eriskay during the war when it was on its way to Jamaica with a cargo of whisky. About 250,000 bottles of whisky were 'liberated' and they are still being found I believe all over the islands, and we have two of the original bottles here as well'.

Fiona added, 'Nothing has really changed in the house since Margaret and John died; it's a home, not a museum, it definitely still feels lived in, it's like Margaret has just gone out to hang out the washing'.

Dónal with Fiona Mackenzie at Canna House.

John Lorne Campbell & Margaret Fay Shaw

Born in Argyll in the west of Scotland in 1906 John Lorne Campbell was one of the most important collectors of traditional folklore and music of Scotland. He lived on the island of Barra in the 1930s where he became friends with the author and Scottish nationalist Compton Mackenzie.

On the island of South Uist in the Outer Hebrides he met the American musician Margaret Fay Shaw and together they bought the small island of Canna in the Small Isles in 1938.

Campbell and Shaw were early environmentalists and farmed on the island for more than forty years as well as writing and recording extensively on the Gaelic culture of the west of Scotland and the Highlands.

Their work produced one of the most important collections of materials on Gaelic Scottish culture in the world including songs, tunes, poetry and a wealth of other material. Campbell donated the island to the National Trust for Scotland in 1981. He died in 1996 while on holiday in Italy where he was first buried but his body was later returned to Canna. Margaret continued to live at Canna House and died there in 2004 at the age of 101.

Loch Hartabhagh

Skye

Skye, probably the most famous of all Scottish islands and home to some of Scotland's most dramatic scenery, is the largest of the Inner Hebrides and it still has a significant Gaelic-speaking population and the locals here are proud of their Celtic heritage.

Skye is also home to Sabhal Mòr Ostaig, the National Centre for Gaelic Culture and Language. The college plays a leading role in promoting Gaelic arts and culture and hosts a programme of artist residencies.

In 2015 the famous Galician piper Carlos Núñez came here for ten days to work on a project called The Atlantic Corridor that was performed at Celtic Connections in Glasgow. The project explored the musical connections along the Atlantic corridor between the Celtic nations.

Dr Decker Forrest, programme leader for Gaelic and Traditional Music at the college and an accomplished piper himself worked on the project with Núñez. Dr Forrest is an expert on the highland bagpipes and is convinced that the

Skye landscape.

Dónal joining a session on the Isle of Skye.

Atlantic played a key role in the development of music and culture in the Celtic world:

'The evidence is to be found in the wider theory of an Atlantic corridor in which many different people from a very wide area were connected culturally and through shared linguistic origins from a very early period.

Our earliest images of the highland bagpipe that exist, in for example architectural relief and sculpture, depict an instrument which is closer to the Spanish gaita than any other pipe that we know of today.'

In a small way Sabhal Mòr Ostaig played its own part in continuing that ancient connection with the project in 2015.

'Carlos had been inspired by a book that had come out written by Hugh Cheape, where Hugh made the hypothesis that the origins of the highland bagpipe are to be found in the piping tradition of northern Spain and Galicia.

Carlos was here for a couple of weeks and used our resources and library and spent a lot of time speaking with myself and Hugh and the result of all this was a fantastic piece of work that could be best described as a Celtic concerto.'

Dr Forrest showed Dónal just how easily a primitive pipe could be made producing a playable instrument simply made from local reeds.

Dr Decker Forrest at Sabhal Mòr Ostaig.

'This is the type of thing we would see throughout the Celtic nations, it isn't unique to just the Highlands of Scotland. It's a simple instrument and all of the materials you see here, all came from the Isle of Skye, a type of reed that grows by the side of the loch and a piece of barley straw. What I did was take a bit of fencing wire, something that has been around for a long time and heated it in a peat fire and burnt the holes through and that's it.'

Dr Decker Forrest demonstrates a simple Celtic pipe at Sabhal Mòr Ostaig.

Joining local musicians for a session on the Isle of Skye.

Such instruments were probably being made thousands of years ago but the development of the iconic highland bagpipe came much later.

'The highland bagpipe became established around about the sixteenth century or the end of the fifteenth century and that's a time of great chaos in the Highlands. It was when the Lordship of the Isles broke down and so you had clans who were fighting constantly to increase their territories.

As we all know the highland bagpipe is particularly well-suited to warfare and has had associations with the army and so on; but very soon the bagpipe and its music became very diverse and for example it became established as a very important instrument for dance music.

Over the centuries a number of different musical traditions within the Highlands of Scotland influenced the highland bagpipe and vice versa. So we have for example instrumental traditions and vocal traditions that attempt to imitate the complex ornaments and so on that are characteristic of the highland bagpipes and also we have repertoire going back and forth between these traditions so they are absolutely inter-mixed.'

Dr Forrest sees this highland tradition as part of a Celtic heritage but also something unique to the area. He sees Celtic music as a broad family of many different styles and traditions.

'A term like Celtic music or Celtic art, they are terms to me that are something similar to say 'African music' or 'south-east Asian music'. They are very useful for those who want to promote and emphasize the broad connections over a lot of people, over a large area. I think in actual fact they tend to wash over the more important, individual and complex features of different musical traditions.

I think that would be the view of a lot of musicians who are often asked to define their music, I think that is very much the case with the highland bagpipe and other bagpipe traditions as well.'

Christine Primrose is one of Scotland's most renowned Gaelic singers and also teaches at Sabhal Mòr Ostaig. A native of the Isle of Lewis, Christine says that there are a variety of songs and themes she has noticed that recur in the music of different Celtic regions such as the murder ballad as was also noted by Mairéad Ní Mhaonaigh in Donegal:

'It exists in various countries, this theme of the two women, one being jealous of the other. In Scottish Gaelic we have it in various forms. There are four or five versions, Lewis lays claim to it, Uist lays claim to it, and Skye and I think it's heard in Nova Scotia, I think it has been found in one of the collections there and Ireland of course.'

Christine believes it is that closeness to the people that makes the music 'traditional' but even so it is always changing and evolving.

'I think in traditional music there is a common thread, because of that fact that it is traditional, it is from the people, it is of the people, it's of the land, it's an oral tradition. It is really like a record of events of how people were feeling all

A good crowd on the Isle of Skye!

Christine Primrose.

through the generations and that is what we find in the songs. They take on what was happening with each generation, they add to them, some bits are lost, some bits are added. It was never broken, put it that way, it just evolves with each generation.'

A proud Scottish Gaelic singer, Christine sees the music as very much relevant today and is confident it will prosper in the future.

'I'm a Scottish Gaelic singer, there are Irish Gaelic singers, Cornish singers or Breton singers; why are they not called 'traditional' Breton singers? I think we're not being fair to the public, to the audiences, I think we should educate them as well.

I think it's shown that the power behind the songs, without any help from outside forces, by government or local councils, up until now we've done without them and we still have the songs. It has never been a broken tradition, and the songs have still survived and with the songs we'll always have the language as well.'

From Sabhal Mòr Ostaig we head west across the stunning landscape of the Isle of Skye to Dunvegan on the west coast.

Here we are in one of the heartlands of Scottish piping and an area steeped in music and Gaelic culture. The one thing that is clear already is that wherever you go, the music never stays the same. It is always changing, evolving, absorbing new influences and here on Skye one group in particular are taking Celtic music in entirely new directions.

Formed in 1991 the Peatbog Faeries have brought Celtic music to a whole new audience in Scotland. Dónal met with piper Peter Morrison and bass player Innes Hutton who explained how the Peatbogs evolved and their roots in the local tradition on Skye.

Peter said, 'Sometimes when you're writing tunes for the Peatbogs, not all of them are like you would write a tune for a trad band. Most of the tracks would work as trad tunes as well.

Peter Morrison and Innes Hutton from the Peatbog Faeries.

We play some of them in sessions. The actual traditional music is really important to me and the traditional tunes are really important to me. This area that we are from, especially the Dunvegan area is one of the most famous places in Scotland for pipes. It's a very important part of our identity as much as anything else.'

Innes is positive about the future of Scottish music and notes that the scene has transformed from when he was a youngster, 'When I was a kid the only traditional music I ever saw on telly was Jimmy Shand, bales of hay, that was it, that was all that was put on telly. Even the good guys that were around in the day like Dick Gaughan, you didn't see them on television and as a young player you didn't get to see the best. I see a lot of the youngsters coming out of the Conservatoire every year and they are really pretty hardcore traditional players and they are very protective of their own regional identities. Festivals like Celtic Connections have completely

With Christine Primrose at Sabhal Mòr Ostaig.

Profile – Christine Primrose

Originally from the Isle of Lewis in the Outer Hebrides, Christine Primrose is widely regarded as one of the greats of Scottish Gaelic singing. A native speaker Christine is a multi-award winning artist winning Gold in Sean-nós at the Royal National Mòd in 1974 and being named Gaelic Singer of the Year at the Scottish Traditional Music Awards in 2009.

Christine was one of the first internationally renowned Scottish Gaelic singers of the modern era having performed across the world.

Her 1982 album *Àite mo Ghaoil* brought Scottish Gaelic singing to a much wider audience at home and abroad.

A broadcaster and teacher she now lives on the Isle of Skye where she teaches Gaelic song at Sabhal Mòr Ostaig. She also continues to record and tour.

changed the perception of trad music for young people.'

Peter added, 'Fifteen years ago I felt a lot of the young traddies were trying too hard, all looking for an angle, not playing enough trad tunes. In the last five years I've felt that a lot of these players seem to have a lot more respect for the actual traditional music. They are teaching constantly and I'm saying 'stop teaching everybody', because eventually the pubs are just going to be full of musicians and there will only be three punters who can't play a tune, that's the way it's going!'

When you look out over this beautiful landscape it's hard to ignore the similarities between Scotland and Ireland. The very landscape itself seems to continue on, on either side of the sea. The terrain is littered with standing stones, brochs and dolmens that could be equally at home in County Clare or Kerry.

The music carries on too, across the sea, telling the same stories, singing the same songs and playing the same melodies with just enough variation here and there to remind you that this is Scotland.

Here in Scotland you also get a sense of how the pipes are an integral part of Celtic music and perhaps the very first instruments to be exported along this Atlantic highway from 1,000 miles away.

There is no doubt that the connections between these two ancient lands are strong and enduring. Now it's time to follow the Celtic Songlines south to the disparate lands of Man, Wales and Cornwall.

Profile – Peatbog Faeries

Formed in 1991 on the Isle of Skye the Peatbog Faeries began life gigging in pubs around Scotland but soon grew a loyal and appreciative fan base. The combination of traditional instruments and tunes with a modern approach soon led the band to be in great demand at festivals near and far.

In 2016 this iconic Scottish band celebrated their twenty-fifth anniversary receiving the Hands Up for Trad, Landmark Award.

Their eighth album *Blackhouse* was nominated for Scottish traditional album of the year in 2015 and they are two-time winners of the Live Act of the Year at the Scottish Traditional Music Awards.

Having played right across the world from Europe to Africa, Asia, North America and Australia they are still going strong with pipe and whistle player and founder member Peter Morrison having played in every gig!

Celtic Crossroads

The Celtic world was defined by the sea. From the craggy coasts and islands of Scotland to the wild Atlantic west of Ireland. The Celts were maritime peoples, trading in goods, language, culture and ideas and of course music.

We have already seen how the ideas and music of the Celts connect Ireland and Scotland. On the next stage of Dónal's journey we head south to the Isle of Man, Wales and Cornwall, to the crossroads of the Celtic world. It was here that Gael met Breton, here that the influences of the Celtic world converged from north, south, east and west.

It is here that you get a real sense of just how important the sea was to the very idea of being a Celt. You hear it in the music too, in the songs and tunes that speak of the sea and the ocean, that long for distant shores.

Echoes of the past on the Isle of Man.

Scenery on the Isle of Man.

Nowhere is the importance of the sea in the Celtic consciousness more apparent than here on the Isle of Man. Here it is all around you, in the sound of the crashing waves breaking on a green, lush landscape that would have felt so familiar to travellers from across the Celtic nations.

Here you will find Neolithic and Bronze Age monuments that would be equally at home in Brittany, Scotland or Ireland. Some believe that the island is named for the mythical Manannán mac Lir who is said to have travelled the oceans of the Celtic world on his sea-borne chariot.

The island acts like the lynchpin of the Celtic landscape, surrounded on all sides by its Celtic cousins, connected to them by the sea. It is like a steppingstone from Gaelic to the Brythonic, a Celtic crossroads in the Irish Sea, to the west beyond St Patrick's Isle is Ireland, to the north Scotland, to which the island once belonged, and to the south

Wales and Cornwall.

Andrew Johnson is an archaeologist with Manx National Heritage, an expert on the island's history he sees the Celtic imprint here as very much one of an evolving culture:

'The Celtic history of the Isle of Man is really about continuity and communication, about the spreading of ideas and technology amongst populations that are largely indigenous. In many ways we think of it as the Iron Age, we are talking about a period from about 500 BC through to the arrival of the Vikings in ninth century.

During that time we see a culture that is very strong, inward-looking in many ways, quite self-contained. They built hill forts, promontory forts around the coastline, they lived in roundhouses. We don't really know much about how they buried their dead, we really know more about how they lived. In many ways it's the story of the Iron Age throughout northern and western Britain and indeed into Europe.'

Andrew believes that what is generally described as Celtic is essentially an Iron Age culture that was pre-eminent in Europe during this period.

'From the Bronze Age what you see is a continuity, the same people are here but new individuals, new ideas, new technology is constantly arriving on the island and that's reflected in the change from a culture that relied primarily on bronze implements to one that began to rely on iron implement from the fifth century BC onwards.'

When it comes to music the record is barren with no archaeological finds of instruments as yet on the island.

'Unfortunately we are bereft, we have no musical instruments from this period at all. The reason that we don't have these things is perhaps a reflection of the environment that we live in. The soils are very acidic and materials like bone and wood are not easily preserved and we are talking about a period that is around about 2,000 years ago.'

He believes that while the Manx culture is strong, it is not always popularly recognised as Celtic.

'The Manx cultural identity is something that I think is very strong and it's also something that is very individual. They perhaps don't always equate that specifically with being Celtic, they perhaps don't always appreciate what the word Celtic means and as an archaeologist the word Celtic can be of limited use.'

Manx musician Tom Callister who we first met in Glasgow does believe that the Manx Celtic identity is coming to the fore and language and music is an essential part of that:

'There are a lot of people on the Isle of Man who are really hardworking cultural stalwarts, who haven't ever let go of what we have on the island and through their ridiculously hard work over the last thirty or forty years there has really been a massive boost, especially to the music and the language on the Isle of Man.

Archaeologist Andrew Johnson.

Manx music is largely unexplored in a way, people have always played it but we have this kind of raw source material on the island, some of the tunes have probably never been played off of the island. I don't think there are any historical recordings of Manx music but with the language there is for sure. Éamon de Valera sent over people to record Manx on big wax cylinders and that became a massively valuable resource.'

On the south coast sits Castletown, and towering over us is the impressive Castle Rushen, a medieval reminder of the island's sometimes violent past. The island's location in the Irish Sea has meant that it has always attracted visitors from near and far; sometimes welcome and sometimes not but they have all left their mark here.

Dr Breesha Maddrell is a musician and is Director of Culture Vannin, the body responsible for promoting the indigenous Manx culture:

'Culture Vannin is actually part of the government, we are a charity and we are tasked with promoting Manx culture, Manx language, music and dance, history, archaeology, everything.'

For her there is a definite sense that Manx music is on the up.

'When I was at school we wouldn't have been taught many Manx songs, we would have just known ones like 'Ellan Vannin' and the Manx national anthem, things like that, or 'The Laxey Wheel' and other popular songs in English.

Nowadays children have the opportunity to learn songs in Manx, they have Manx dancing, it's much more open to people and we've got a lot of resources available online as well so everyone has a chance to learn. It has just grown in popularity and with some of the professional bands coming through, people like Tom Callister playing with Barrule and Mec Lir, so it's great.'

The growth in Celtic festivals and the wider music scene has also been of huge benefit to Manx music according to Breesha giving the island a confidence in its place at the heart of a wide Celtic world.

'The festivals here are one of the ways that we learn about other Celtic cultures and the way we show off our own culture when we go elsewhere. That certainly increases the number of people who are interested in Manx music and Manx language but also the standard as well because you get to see what other people are doing and you want to do it a little bit better than them!'

As elsewhere Manx culture is also evolving with these new influences and Breesha believes that evolution is essential for the tradition to survive.

'I think it's a really fundamental part of the tradition, if you don't take the songs and the tunes to make them your own then you're not really being true to the tradition. I've been fortunate enough to play in a band with Aalin Clague for a

Castle Rushen.

With Breesha Maddrell at Castle Rushen.

We have strong links with Wales because we like singing in harmony, we have strong links with Ireland because we are a lost island and we are also connected to Scotland and the Western Isles through the Norse, through the Kingdom of Man and the Isles. We now have strong links with Glasgow where some of our young people are training and playing there at the Conservatoire.'

These age-old links are also apparent in the music, as we have seen in Scotland and Ireland.

'I think the more obvious links are in the tunes, because once you have a song, you have words. If they are in Manx Gaelic they might have been carried to Scotland, as we think 'Ushag Veg Ruy' was, and we would borrow songs from Ireland and they become part of our tradition.

I think that's what is great about Celtic music, it's that movement of tunes and songs and what you make them when they are in one place, that is what's important. The way we play things and the way we sing things here makes it Manx.'

As well as its strong musical traditions the island is also

long time and she is somebody I would say would embody that, taking an old song and just stretch it out and play with it and make it your own. I think the tradition has to have that, it has to have conservative elements and innovative elements and it's the tension between the two that keeps it alive.'

As for the island's Celtic cultural identity it seems to be reflected by its geographical position at the centre of the Celtic world.

'Because we are an island in the middle of everything we always like to say that we are at the heart of the Celtic world because we've got the other countries all around us. The sea has been a pathway in the past, it has not been a barrier so we look to the west, to the east, to the south, in every direction.

We've been ruled by different people at different times, the Scottish and the Irish have fought over us, as have the English; we've had a strong Methodist tradition. So all of these different things link us to the other countries.

Manx singer Aalin Clague recording for *The Celtic Songlines.*

Profile – Barrule

Probably the best-known traditional act to come out of the Isle of Man in recent years Barrule consists of fiddle player Tom Callister, accordionist Jamie Smith and accompanist Adam Rhodes.

Named for the mythical mountain on the island where the Celtic god Manannán mac Lir is said to have built his fortress. Barrule are known for their energetic contemporary style all the while holding true to the proud tradition of Manx music.

With a growing international reputation and two well-received albums already under their belt they embarked on a tour of the USA in 2017.

Other major appearances include Celtic Connections, WOMAD, Festival Interceltique de Lorient, La Grande Rencontre in Montreal, Orkney Folk Festival and the National Celtic Festival in Melbourne.

Breesha Maddrell.

home to its own unique style of traditional dancing, notably Celtic but also distinctly Manx as leading local dancer Gráinne Joughin explains:

'For anyone who has never seen Manx dancing before, the best way to explain it would be, Have you seen Scottish dancing? Have you seen Irish Dancing? It's kind of half way between the two really.

It's a freer style of dancing is the only thing that I would say, Irish and Scottish dancing have become much more of a competitive game whereas Manx dancing has stayed quite true to the social aspect so in that sense it is a little bit freer, there are less rules if you like.

There were certainly two figures in Manx dancing who were very prominent and responsible for the revival, Mona Douglas in the 1920s and shortly afterwards Leighton Stowell who were both very involved with getting Manx dancing back up onto its feet.'

Now enjoying a revival on the island Gráinne sees the dancing and music of the Isle of Man as inextricably linked.

'I think they come hand in hand, there is a great opportunity for musicians to play for dancers and equally in return you can't dance without musicians, they go together, they are one thing.'

It's been fascinating to see here on the Isle of Man how even the smallest of the Celtic nations has been able to support and sustain its own musical culture. Now we take to the sea again, this time heading south to Wales where a vibrant and individual Celtic culture has existed for centuries.

Song – 'Car Ny Ferrishyn' (Fairy Dance)

'The Fairy Dance' is one of the best known reels identified with the Isle of Man and has been played in a number of versions and variations dating from the beginning of the nineteenth century. Possibly a variation of an original Scottish tune it was published by the Manx folklorist Mona Douglas in the 1950s. The Manx version was popular on the island long before this however and the tune is a good example of one that has been passed on through the oral tradition resulting in a variety of similar versions in different Celtic countries.

Most likely originally played on the fiddle, a harp version became common on the Isle of Man in the twentieth century.

Gráinne Joughin Manx dancing accompanied by Jamie Smith.

A Land of Song

From the Isle of Man we take to the sea again and head south to Wales and for the first time on our journey we are in the traditional homeland of the Brythonic Celts. Most historians agree that virtually all of what is now England and Wales was once the home of Brythonic Celtic people. Some include the Picts of Scotland as part of this broad Brythonic group.

The Celts of England however had to contend with multiple invasions from Romans, Saxons, Vikings and Normans, who eventually all but eradicated Celtic culture from central, southern and eastern Britain. The famous Queen Boudica, who led a failed rebellion against Roman rule in AD 60, a member of the British Celtic tribe the Iceni, was from modern day Norfolk in the east of England.

Pushed further west, the mountainous terrain of Wales

Anglesey, Wales.

Meeting harpist Llio Rhydderch on Anglesey.

offered some refuge for this once proud British Celtic culture and it was here in Wales that the Brythonic Celts of Britain, the Britons, finally managed to preserve their cultural heritage.

In the twelfth century the famous chronicler Giraldus Cambrensis (Gerald of Wales) wrote extensively on his native land and noted that even at this time the Welsh were renowned for their singing. He described 'their rhymed songs' as 'subtle and ingenious', while also noting, 'the Welsh go to extremes in all matters, you may never find anyone worse than a bad Welshman, but you will certainly never find anyone better than a good one'.

Welsh folk or traditional music is believed to have had much in common with its counterparts in Scotland and Ireland but, unlike those areas, Wales came under the influence of

Methodism in the eighteenth and nineteenth centuries. The Methodists did not look kindly on much of the traditional folk music of the time resulting in choral music and hymns becoming far more popular.

Despite this, one of the strongest musical traditions in all of the Celtic countries did manage to survive in Wales, that of the Welsh or triple harp – the national instrument of Wales. It originated in Italy but has a long tradition in Wales going back several hundred years, with the oldest written harp music in Europe coming from Wales.

To find out more we have come to Ynys Môn (Anglesey), the largest island of Wales. Once a stronghold of the Druids and also home to an Irish colony, the island was among the last refuges of the ancient Celtic Britons. The Romans invaded in AD 60 and finally conquered the island in AD 77 – its copper reserves too valuable to ignore – but Anglesey has never forgotten its Celtic heritage.

Anglesey is the home of Llio Rhydderch one of the foremost exponents of the famed Welsh harp. Together with her former teacher Nansi Richards, Llio is credited with keeping the tradition of the Welsh harp alive in the twentieth century. A talented musician, she can trace her own lineage in the Welsh harp stretching back to the fourteenth century. Now a teacher herself, she has seen the triple harp enjoy a resurgence in popularity.

Like much Celtic music generally, the survival of the Welsh harp is due in large part to the oral tradition. According to Llio, 'The oral tradition is how I picked up everything really, Nansi Richards used to come to our home and she'd pass on these tunes to me. That is the way that I was taught, and that is the way that I'm teaching.'

Despite the harp being the national symbol of Ireland and with some of the oldest examples coming from Scotland, it was in Wales that the tradition survived to the modern era. 'The Irish tradition was broken, where as our tradition is unbroken,' said Llio, 'and here on Anglesey we can go back to the 1300s. So it is an unbroken tradition and it is continuing, thank goodness.'

Llio is also optimistic that a new generation of harpists will keep the tradition alive, 'There are a few of us who are passing it on, but expecting it to develop. You hope that the pupils then will work on their own as I was encouraged to do in the early days. You have the tune, now make something which is personal to yourself from it.'

With more than 1,600 miles of coastline and a mainly mountainous interior, Wales has always looked to the sea and nowhere more so than on the beautiful Llŷn Peninsula in north Wales, just down the coast from Anglesey.

Above and right: Meeting harpist Llio Rhydderch on Anglesey.

Much like the west of Ireland, this area's unspoilt remoteness has seen Celtic culture and tradition endure. It is a stronghold of the Welsh language, the most widely spoken of all the modern Celtic languages and the 30-mile-long peninsula is dotted with archaeological reminders of its ancient heritage.

A reconstructed Celtic roundhouse at the Felin Uchaf centre on the Llŷn Peninsula.

Here we find the Felin Uchaf Centre a fifteen-year project nearing completion that aims to bring some of those ancient structures to life.

At Felin Uchaf Dónal met with local historian, archaeologist, broadcaster and musician Rhys Mwyn who explained:

'This is what we would call a round house, where people lived during what we call the Celtic period, the example here is slightly larger than usual. Normally they are about eight metres wide, which suggests some of them may well have been gathering places.'

What kind of music might have been played in such gathering places is harder to determine however, as we have found elsewhere instruments from the period are hard to come by.

'The problem in terms of archaeology is that musical instruments rarely survive, so if they had whistles or string instruments, the chances of those being found today are slim. But I think obviously in Wales we can say we were choral singing, I'm sure we were!'

In Wales the traditions handed down have been adapted and taken on by a new generation in perhaps a more dynamic way than elsewhere, as Rhys explained, 'What's happened in Wales really is that our generation and subsequent generations have taken the traditional and the now, and I would argue that what we have created are modern folk songs but we've plugged it in, it's a bit Bob Dylan!

We were politicised by the punk movement and what it suggested to us is that we need to shout out a bit more loudly and clearly where Welsh identity stands. For us it was an inspiration; not to copy them, not to translate them. Here in north Wales we have a voice and we can create. I think we always brought in the Welsh traditions with us, but we also brought in a whole new voice. I've never been as optimistic

Rhys Mwyn.

Filming with Dafydd Davies-Hughes at Felin Uchaf.

because we generate such talent, such visionaries.'

One of those new voices belongs to Jamie Smith, a native of south Wales, who has played with Manx trad group Barrule and founded the Inter-Celtic music band Jamie Smith's Mabon. Being brought up in south Wales, playing for Welsh folk dancing that his parents were involved with gave Jamie an early insight into the possibilities of Celtic music:

'I was taken at a young age to the Festival Interceltique de Lorient, so right from an early age I was exposed to this big melting pot of bands and dancing from all the different Celtic countries. I've grown up with this sense that they are connected and I think a lot of people from the Celtic countries love that feeling of connection as well.'

For Jamie the traditional core of the music is still essential and there is a distinction to be made between Mabon's 'Inter-Celtic' approach and 'Celtic-fusion'.

'When I hear the word fusion I think more like the main idea is to bring other styles like jazz or rock in and combine them with traditional tunes.

Although there's nothing wrong with that and it is a large part of what the band does, it's not at the core. The important thing is choosing tunes that you love to play and then deciding how to represent this tune, and let the tune lead the way as much as possible.'

In Wales we have seen how Celtic culture has endured despite the proximity of first Roman and then Anglo Saxon influences. Next we take to the seas again and follow the Celtic Songlines south to probably the most isolated Celtic nation of all, to Cornwall.

Profile – Llio Rhydderch

As a child Llio Rhydderch was taught the harp by Nansi Richards (Telynores Maldwyn) known in her day as the 'Queen of the Welsh Triple Harp', a title which Llio Rhydderch is now increasingly being given herself.

Llio is today one of the most pre-eminent exponents of the traditional Welsh harp and is widely recognised as the foremost and most innovative and influential Welsh harpist. A proud defender of the tradition, she can directly trace to herself through an unbroken line from teacher to pupil from the fourteenth century.

Llio is also an innovator and advocate that the harp remains a living tradition, values she hopes she can pass on to the next generation of Welsh harpists as they were handed down to her.

Profile – Jamie Smith's Mabon

Formed by Welsh accordionist Jamie Smith in 1999 this innovative band started out playing Welsh Celtic dance music in an acoustic quartet of fiddle, accordion, guitar and percussion. Shortly after that Jamie started to experiment with composition, and the traditional Celtic tunes of Mabon's early days gradually made way for his own creations, influenced both by traditional music and by other, more contemporary Celtic artists.

Today Jamie Smith's Mabon is a band that embodies the spirit of Celtic music drawing on influences from across the Celtic world from Scotland to Asturias and all points in between.

The band have so far recorded five albums and have played at some of the biggest Celtic music festivals around the world including WOMAD, Womex, Shetland, Rainforest, Fairport's Cropredy Convention, Hebcelt, Celtic Connections and the Festival Interceltique de Lorient.

Jamie Smith.

Song – 'Llef Harlech'/'Beth Yw'r Haf I Mi'

'Llef Harlech' or 'Harlech's Cry' is a traditional Welsh ballad or lament that probably originated in the seventeenth century but may come from a much older original tune. The German violinist, Johann (John) Baptist Malchair, who collected folk music from across Europe, first noted the tune in the late eighteenth century from where it became popular in Welsh repertoire and was published by the professor of music at Oxford University William Crotch.

A later arrangement 'Beth Yw'r Haf I Mi?' or 'What Is the Summer to Me?' also became popular especially for the harp from the 1960s onwards. This version is also a lament and tells the story of a man who pleads for the return of his lover who has left him. T.H. Parry-Williams and his wife Amy wrote the lyrics in 1963. Williams was a professor of Welsh and noted Celtic scholar who sought to promote his native language and culture through literature and music. A major Welsh poet and author he also sought to strengthen links between the Welsh and Breton speaking communities.

Cornwall

We have followed the coasts south along the ancient trading routes that carried copper, tin and bronze. Those same routes carried culture and music too from Galicia in the south to Scotland in the north and to here in Cornwall.

Cornwall is both Celtic and English and is a reminder that once the Celts were the dominant culture right across Britain and all along this Atlantic coast.

At Cape Cornwall and just to the south of Land's End, we are once again facing the wild Atlantic. This beautiful coastline feels very familiar, very Celtic – further south there are other 'Land's Ends'; Finistère in Brittany, Finisterre in Galicia, all facing west out towards the ocean, all connected by the Celtic Songlines.

Cornwall is littered with mysterious megalithic monuments, particularly to the west of the peninsula, and like its Celtic contemporaries was a firmly established part of the Atlantic trade routes of the Bronze Age. In the Iron Age the Brythonic-speaking peoples of Cornwall maintained close cultural ties

Dónal at Cape Cornwall.

Steve Hartgroves.

with Wales and Brittany at a time when access by sea was often easier than access by land.

It's that proximity to the sea that seems to be the constant in all of the places Dónal is visiting on this journey – it is the sea that enabled Celtic cultures and their music to flourish from north to south.

According to local archaeologist Steve Hartgroves, Cornwall is very much part of that mysterious Atlantic culture that left these huge monuments to remind us of their existence:

'The megalithic culture spreads along the western fringe of Europe. There are stone circles in Portugal, Spain, Britain, Wales, Ireland and up north to Scandinavia as well. It seems to be a function of the migration of farming technology across Europe.

When it got the Atlantic Ocean, there was nowhere to go and it seems to have turned in on itself, people started to develop these ideas about doing things with very large chunks of rock!'

There are also clues to the links with other areas in artefacts that have been found in Cornwall.

'I think if we were looking for evidence of a link to Ireland the most obvious thing is the gold work, there are four lunulae that have been discovered in Cornwall and at least one of them it has been suggested was an 'Irish type' pattern.

The megaliths in Brittany are quite different from the ones in Cornwall, but quite similar in many ways to the ones in Ireland. They share decorative motifs, circles, zig-zags and chevrons with the Boyne Valley ones and I'm sure that they were in contact with each other. Goods were moving around at this time, traded from Cornwall all over southern England and northern England as well.'

Not far from Land's Ends is the workshop of musician and uilleann pipe maker Alan Burton. A native Cornishman, how did he end up making uilleann pipes?

'I was played the album *Well Below the Valley* (Planxty) and it was the piping of Liam O'Flynn. I'd been listening to a lot of bagpipe music and gaida music from Bulgaria but this had an essence to it, a voice that spoke a lot deeper.

I quit my job and used my holiday pay to buy myself a practice set of pipes. Being far away from the centre of traditional Irish music and piping, maintaining the pipes was a big problem for me and needs must meant that I ended up learning to make reeds.'

Alan didn't stop there however and has since become a sought after pipe maker well beyond Cornwall.

'It turned out that I'm quite good at reed making and for the piper the reed is the holy grail. Circumstances ended up offering me the chance to have a go at making some pipes, which I jumped at. I'm currently making a set for Na Piobairi Uilleann in Dublin, the piper's club, which for me is a big honour.'

And what of Cornwall's native pipes, are there any in existence?

'There are Cornish pipes as such which have been redesigned but these have not been made from existing examples historically, these are really from drawings and carvings. Whether the internal parts of the instrument are correct and whether the tuning and the note matrix is correct we don't know.'

We are on the road again, heading to Penzance and the studios of Dare Mason where Dónal is meeting up with Neil Davey and Hilary Coleman.

Neil and Hilary both come from families steeped in Cornish music and culture and through their own band Dalla have been key members in the ongoing revival of Celtic music in Cornwall.

Neil was formerly a member of the seminal Cornish band Bucca while Hilary is one of he foremost singers in the Cornish language today.

For Hilary, Cornwall's tradition is influenced to large degree by the peninsula's geography, 'I think the fact that we are surrounded by water, those influences are inevitable and what

Alan Burton and Dónal Lunny.

Alan Burton.

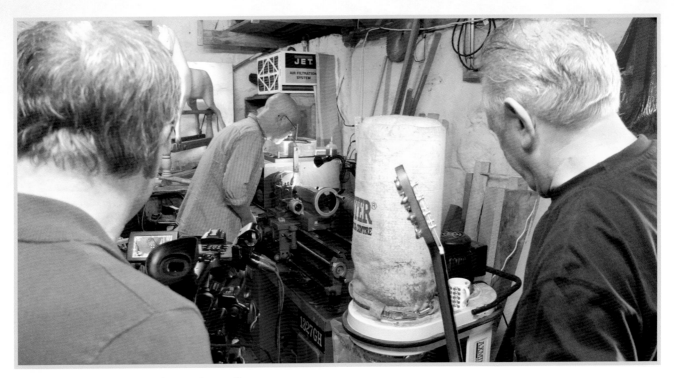

Filming at Alan Burton's workshop in Cornwall.

makes Cornish music quite unique in a way is the combination of all these things. You've got this Breton old modal layer, you've got the major tunes coming in, then you've got the industrial revolution which produced Methodism and the choirs so you've got all this harmony singing and hymns. It's like layers in geology, you layer up, and to get back down to some sort of pure golden age is a bit unrealistic.'

Much like on the Isle of Man, Cornish culture and its sense of Celtic identity has enjoyed a renaissance since the folk revival of the 1970s. The Cornish language, which is closest to Breton among the Celtic languages, is also enjoying a revival and once again we see that the fortunes of the culture, language and music are inextricably linked.

From here we follow the Celtic Songlines south again, this time to the continent, to Brittany and Galicia.

Dónal with Neil Davey and Hilary Coleman.

Hilary Coleman.

Recording for *The Celtic Songlines* at Dare Mason's studios in Cornwall.

The Kings Arms, St Just.

St Just, Cornwall.

Song – 'Delkiow Syvy'

'Delkiow Syvy' or the 'Strawberry Leaves' is a traditional Cornish folk song that tells the story of a young girl who goes to pick strawberry leaves that are said to bestow beauty. On the way she meets a young tailor who tries to charm the young girl to become his lover.

The song is certainly very old and the Cornish folk singer Brenda Wootton had claimed it was the only original Cornish folk song to survive into the modern era. This view has been disputed with some claiming the song may originally have an English origin.

Whatever its true origin, today it is among the most popular of traditional Cornish songs.

Profile – Dalla

Formed in 1999 Dalla are the leading contemporary Celtic music group playing in Cornwall today. The families of original members Neil Davey and Hilary Coleman have both been deeply involved in the revival of Celtic Cornish culture that began in earnest in the 1970s.

Dalla uses driving bouzouki and mandolin with clarinet melodies which gives the band a distinctive Cornish sound. It was Neil's older brother Merv who collected much of the Cornish repertoire in the 1970s and together with his other two brothers Andy and Kyt they formed the groundbreaking traditional Cornish band Bucca who released the highly influential album *An Tol an Pedn an Telynor* in 1980.

Dónal with Neil Davey.

Dalla.

Neil went on to become a member of the Inter-Celtic group Anam in the 1990s with members from the UK and Ireland, before forming Dalla.

Hilary's family have been equally influential promoting Cornish language and music and she was previously a member of Gwaryoryon, a Cornish band influenced by the early success of Bucca, as well as The Jack and Jenny Band and she is a member of the Cornwall Songwriters. She continues to be actively involved in numerous events promoting Cornish music, dance and language.

BREIZH

Brittany

Brittany is a rugged peninsula jutting out into the Atlantic, and home to more than four million people. With its many rocky bays and secluded harbours the coast extends more than 1,700 miles. Surrounded by the Atlantic on three sides, this is the home of the last major Celtic culture in continental Europe.

The Bretons are descendants of Britons who established a new home here more than 1,400 years ago as they fled from the encroaching Saxons in Britain. It was a natural choice, the area was already home to some of the last of the Gauls, the Celtic peoples of France who had traded tin and bronze across the oceans with Cornwall and Wales for centuries.

The reminders of the Celtic past are everywhere and the connections with the other Celtic nations are plain to see in the landscape itself. Mont Saint-Michel, reputedly founded by an Irish hermit stands gatekeeper to the Breton lands just across the border in Normandy, the parent of St Michael's Mount in Cornwall – two monuments to the close connections between these areas.

Dónal in Brittany.

Harpers in Dinan.

Laoise Kelly.

Alan Stivell.

When the Britons came here they brought their language with them and it survives to this day, spoken by some 200,000 people, and with language comes music. Brittany has been at the heart of the revival in Celtic music and the very phrase was first coined here. Today there is a vibrant and growing traditional music scene in Brittany with the harp and the pipes central to the unique Breton sound.

In the beautiful city of Dinan every year musicians from across the world come together to celebrate that most Celtic of instruments, the harp. The city is home to the Maison de la Harpe, whose mission is to promote the playing and enjoyment of the Celtic harp across the world.

The harp has been played in Ireland, Scotland, Wales and Brittany for hundreds of years. The harp may be Ireland's national symbol but it is here in Brittany that the tradition was kept alive as it declined elsewhere. Today the harp is central to

Breton music and is enjoying a revival right across the Celtic nations and every summer the festival attracts some of the top harpists from across the world.

One of them is Irish harpist Laoise Kelly from Westport. Laoise now lives on Achill Island on Ireland's west coast and has been playing the harp since she was a child. According to Laoise the harp is in a stronger position now in Ireland than it has been for generations:

'The harp was the dominant instrument in Ireland for centuries, it went through all the history of the country with politics; in 1597 the law of the land was 'hang the harpers and destroy their instruments,' and that was the law of the land for eight years because the harpers held so much power in society. I think we are literally coming back from that time and it has never been stronger than it is now especially in the last thirty years.'

She believes that there are strong similarities and connections among the harping traditions of the Celtic countries.

'We'd have similar rhythms, so we'd have the suantraí, geantraí, goltraí. Goltraí are lullabies, the music for sleeping; geantraí is the happy, celebratory music and dancing music and goltraí which would be laments and music for grieving. In ancient times the harper wasn't a proper harper unless you could play the three strains.

Our traditions are similar, especially if you go back a couple of hundred years but nowadays we have the Celtic harp or the Irish harp and the Welsh traditional harp is the triple harp and Llio Rhydderch of course would be the queen of that instrument.'

Festivals like Dinan have been very important to fostering those links in recent years as she explained.

'There are a growing number of harp festivals. There is a huge connection between Ireland, Scotland, Wales, Brittany and Galicia. It's intuitive and natural and it's easy to pick up their music, the same as we would learn a tune, a jig or a reel, it's easy to sit down and learn a gavotte or one of the Galician tunes. At harp festivals like Dinan it's amazing to meet up because we're the same, it's an easy connection, like a language. Also in faerie law, the music from the faeries is common to all our Celtic traditions.'

Laoise also singles out Breton harper Alan Stivell for his unique contribution to the revival of Celtic music, not just the harp.

'Alan Stivell is the most important and influential harper there is, and musician across all of Celtic music. He has influenced a whole wave of musicians, not just harpists. He would have influenced the movement in Ireland in the 1970s, the Bothy Band, the emergence of Planxty and these kind of bands. The culture was repressed but now we have a chance to celebrate, it feels like it's in its heyday now; the connection is strong and it's unique to our Celtic countries.'

With the success of Celtic festivals in Brittany and Scotland, Laoise believes that more can be done in Ireland to foster these connections.

'Considering our modern day small world that is getting smaller, we could definitely do more with bringing our Celtic cultures together. Certain events like Lorient in Brittany and Celtic Connections in Glasgow are huge, but definitely in Ireland we could do more to showcase our Celtic cousins and how similar they are and show the Irish people.'

From Dinan we head to Lorient on Brittany's south coast. This bustling port city is home to the Festival Interceltique.

From humble beginnings in the early 1970s it has grown to become one of the biggest cultural festivals in the world attracting more than 800,000 visitors and musicians and artists from across the globe. There is no better place to witness the community of Celtic music.

Nearby lives a legend of the Celtic music revival. Alan

The Festival Interceltique in Lorient.

Breton chanteuse Kohann recording for *The Celtic Songlines*.

Dónal at the Festival Interceltique in Lorient.

The appreciative crowd at Dónal's gig at the Festival Interceltique in Lorient.

Performers at the Festival Interceltique in Lorient.

Stivell is a harpist and multi-instrumentalist who has been at the forefront of exploring the connections between the music of the Celtic nations for more than fifty years.

He is credited with first describing music as 'Celtic' in the 1960s and has also been a pioneer in taking the music in new directions:

'I was nine-years-old when my father made the first Celtic harp in Brittany for centuries, the Celtic harp is something that is not traditional in Brittany, it was very aristocratic in fact. It is remembering the time when Brittany was an independent country where even the dukes and counts were still speaking some Breton.

So we have to go back very far in the past, we have to go back to the time where we can consider that the music and the harp itself had something Celtic in it still. If we are Irish or Breton we are something different from French or English. I'm sure that this influence goes into the way we play, the way we even might draw something.'

For Alan it has always been about supporting the culture of Brittany and maintaining its distinctiveness.

'When my father made that first Celtic harp it was at a time of the first steps of a revival in Brittany. I began to be professional as a singer in fact mainly, even though I was too shy to sing before; hidden behind my harp it was easier to sing and I began to get known and even a bit famous very quickly in fact from the mid 1960s to the very early 1970s, it came very quickly.

So then I did *Reflections*, then *Renaissance of the Celtic Harp* and then the Olympia in Paris, which was a big success but at the same time I wanted to take advantage of being popular. Nobody knows better Celtic culture, Breton culture in France so it was very important.

I never had in mind to become famous myself, I wanted to make my culture famous. I think many musicians are almost shy in that way because they would say that they are too proud

Performers at the Festival Interceltique in Lorient.

Meeting the legendary Alan Stivell.

to promote themselves. I think there is this feeling in many Breton musicians, if many people are a fan of Breton music there is less chance that Breton culture will die.'

With the festival at Lorient in full swing Dónal also meets with an old friend Sylvain Barou and joined him on stage for an impromptu gig.

A gifted flautist, Sylvain also plays the uilleann pipes and is a respected player of both Breton and Irish music.

For Sylvain the influence of the new wave of bands coming out of Ireland, a movement of which Dónal was very much a part, were crucial in giving momentum to the revival in Brittany:

'Celtic music for me has a special meaning, the meaning of travelling. I think in Irish music there was a kind of revolution in the 1970s and Breton music got it as well, but in a different way.

Thanks to festivals like this, since the beginning in the 1960s and 1970s we've been able to meet other musicians; that has influenced our music very much. Well-known musicians toured a lot here in the 1970s and we were influenced very much by

Sylvain Barou.

this, it influenced us in the way we used the instruments and the way we arranged music.'

It's almost time to leave Lorient but before we go Dónal wants to meet with Lisardo Lombardía the director of the festival here.

Lisardo is a native of Asturias in northern Spain and first came to Lorient as part of the Asturian delegation in 1985, he has been the director of the festival here since 2007.

How important does he feel the festival has been to the revival in Celtic music in Brittany and beyond?

'I think that Celtic music in Brittany is more and more alive, and very open to creation. There is a new generation, who have big ideas and are introducing new aesthetics, there is great freedom now in Brittany.

I think for the future we have to banish the idea that Celtic music is not part of the new way, our future is our present.'

Here in Brittany you get a real sense that people take

On stage with Sylvain Barou at the Festival Interceltique in Lorient.

pride in their Celtic heritage; it is something that is very much part of their identity.

Konan Mevel is a piper and member of the band Skilda, who much like the Peatbog Fairies in Scotland and Hyper[borea] in Ireland are taking the music in new directions while remaining true to the traditional roots.

Konan brings Dónal to the island of Gavrinis in the Gulf of Morbihan off Brittany's south coast to see a passage tomb that is home to some of the most remarkable neolithic art in Europe; you could call it the Breton Newgrange. He believes that these Neolithic monuments that are common in the Celtic countries are evidence of ancient ties between the different areas:

'When I was a child I started travelling to Celtic countries with my parents, travelling to Wales or Ireland or Cornwall. We would visit these standing stones sites and although they were not built by the Celts they were like a link between the different countries and cultures.

When I travel or visit other sites here in Brittany it reminds me of other sites in Scotland like Callanish or in Ireland like Newgrange. When I go to Newgrange I think about Brittany, I love that, this is really a strong connection I think between the different Celtic countries.'

With his band Skilda Konan also represents the most modern aspects of Celtic music combining the new and the old to continue the culture as an ever evolving and living tradition.

'Skilda is a mix of the Breton culture, the Breton music in a modern way, also Gaelic Waulking songs mixed with techno or electro sounds. I have a feeling that with this band Skilda I'm really part of this Celtic landscape which is a mental landscape as well as a geographic landscape.'

Dónal playing with Konan Mevel at Gavrinis.

Profile – Alan Stivell

One of the leading figures in Celtic music in recent decades, Alan Stivell is a staunch defender of Breton culture and advocate of Celtic music.

Credited as one of the first musicians to describe his music as Celtic he is master harpist as well as a piper and bombard player.

Coming to prominence in the early 1970s Stivell was at the forefront of the revival of harping in Brittany and of a wider revival in Celtic music.

Playing one of the first revival Breton harps made by his father Georges Cochevelou as a child, his interest in Celtic music, folklore, language and mythology led him to become one of the leading proponents of Celtic music.

As well as a staunch defender of the Breton tradition Stivell has been a leading innovator in Celtic music and is often cited as one of the originators of Celtic rock in the 1970s. He has made numerous highly influential albums over the years with his *Renaissance of the Celtic Harp* (1971) perhaps the best known.

He has sold millions of records and has used his success to promote Celtic music as widely as possible having collaborated with a wide range of other musicians ranging from The Chieftains to Youssou N'Dour and Kate Bush.

An accomplished vocalist his sings in Breton, French and Gaelic.

Following the Songlines to the island of Gavrinis, Brittany.

Carnac, Brittany.

Song – 'An Hini A Garan'

'An Hini A Garan' is a traditional Breton gwerz that translates into English as 'The One I Love'. It has become one of the more popular traditional Breton tunes internationally in recent years with several versions and interpretations recorded by a variety of artists in Brittany and beyond.

A gwerz is a Breton form of song that is similar to a ballad or lament that usually tells a story based on mythology or an historical event.

'An Hini A Garan' tells the story of a woman lamenting her lost love who has gone away never to return. It is believed to originate from the town of Vannes on Brittany's south coast.

A 1960 version recorded by Alan Stivell and Andrea Ar Gouilh led to the song becoming popular in the Breton repertoire. Other versions have been recorded by Carlos Núñez, Denez Prigent, Siobhan Owen, Cécile Corbel and many others.

The one I love, one day he left me
Left for distant countries, countries that I don't know
Left for distant countries to earn his bread
Lost, lost one day, the one I love.

Megalithic art at Gavrinis.

Gavrinis, Brittany.

Profile – Kornog

Formed in the early 1980s Kornog (meaning west) are one of the most influential Breton folk groups of the Celtic revival in Brittany.

They recorded four albums during the decade and another in 2000 and while no longer officially together they do still play at occasional concerts and festivals.

Taking inspiration from many of the new wave of Irish bands from the 1970s they are known for their use of bouzouki and mandolin introduced by Scottish member Jamie McMenemy of the Battlefield Band.

As well as enjoying success in Europe, Kornog toured extensively in the United States and the band has led to several related acts comprising some of the members, most notably Pennoù Skoulm.

Song – 'Marv Pontkalleg'

'Marv Pontkalleg' or 'The Death of Pontcallec' is a classic Breton gwerz that tells the story of the Marquis de Pontcallec. The Marquis led the 'Pontcallec conspiracy' against the French crown in 1720.

The conspiracy failed and its leaders including Pontcallec were executed in Nantes. The Marquis subsequently became a folk hero for Breton independence and autonomy.

The song portrays Pontcallec as a champion of the Breton people who is ultimately betrayed and the sadness of the people of Brittany at the failure of the conspiracy.

Many of the major artists in Breton music have recorded versions of the song including Éliane Pronost, Gilles Servat, Tri Yann and Alan Stivell.

Galicia

We are on the final stage of our journey and we've come to Galicia in Spain's far northwest. This area was once home to a thriving Celtic culture and takes its name from the Celtic tribe the Gallaeci.

It is the southern terminus of the Celtic Songlines that carried commerce, culture and music from here to Britain, Ireland and Scotland. There have long been stories of travellers from these parts who made their way north to a fabled island of green pastures where they established a new Celtic homeland. In 2009 researchers in Trinity College Dublin published findings suggesting this story is more than mere myth, showing that people from this part of Spain are closely related to the Irish, especially on the west coast.

What we've learned on this journey is that sometimes you just have to trust your instincts and here in Galicia you just get that feeling that this is indeed a Celtic land. The native language may be long gone but you can still hear those ancient connections in the music and in the voices, you can see it and feel it in the landscape.

When the famous music collector Alan Lomax came here in

Castro de Barona.

Dónal at Castro de Barona, Galicia.

Filming at Castro de Barona.

1952 he was also convinced of that connection, 'Our first trip was down the road towards Vigo. The countryside had that same fey look I had seen only in southern Ireland, although there was really no resemblance in the shape of the hills or the vegetation; but somehow here, too, one could see strange creatures living in the bright green hedgerows.'

At Castro de Barona, an ancient Celtic hill fort not far from Santiago de Compostela you can still imagine how those Celts once lived.

The familiar looking stone huts would not be out of place in Dingle or Donegal and there are numerous surviving examples of this 'Castro Culture' right across northwestern Spain, and some of those buildings are still in use to this day.

It was to places like Castro de Barona here on the Atlantic coast that traders and travellers in pre-Christian times went, west to the ends of the earth – Finisterre, following the stars of the Milky Way on its earthly equivalent, the vía Láctea. Later, Christian pilgrims followed the same routes west to Santiago

Dónal in Santiago de Compostela.

Carlos Núñez.

Dónal tries out some replica medieval instruments at the Irish College in Santiago de Compostela with Carlos Núñez, Esteban Bolado and Pancho Álvarez.

With Carlos Núñez at the Irish College in Santiago de Compostela.

along the Camino to pay their respects to St James who is said to be buried in the city. Irish Christians came too, to the Irish Colleges established across Europe to train Ireland's priests who were persecuted at home following the Tudor conquest.

At 44 Rúa Nova once stood the Irish College of Santiago de Compostela, the second of five such colleges in Spain, established in 1605 as a place of refuge for Irish exiles.

It is here that Dónal is meeting with the famed Galician piper Carlos Núñez. Carlos is a master of the native Galician bagpipe, the gaita. Known to many in Ireland as the 'seventh Chieftain' he has for many years been one of the leading advocates for recognition of a wider Celtic musical culture.

For Carlos the very idea of Celtic music is all about the connections between people, connections that he feels are very real:

'For me, Celtic music is like this Irish College, it is connections; Celtic music makes it possible for people speaking different languages for the music to connect us and I think that comes from thousands of years ago and the sea!'

He feels that Galicia can play a special role in connecting the Iberian Celtic tradition with the Hispanic diaspora, much as Irish and Scottish music has done in North America.

'Maybe Galicia is like the Ireland of the south, it is the door for Celtic music to Latin America. The Hispanic connection in the same way that Irish people and Scottish people emigrated to North America, the Galicians went all over Latin America. We can feel that in the music, in the same way that Irish music and Breton music helped Galicia to recover our tradition, maybe we can help on the Celtic Latin American music to come again.'

At the Irish College in Santiago de Compostela with Carlos Núñez, Esteban Bolado and Pancho Álvarez.

Carlos took part in the 2015 Atlantic Corridor project on the Isle of Skye and this underlined for him the connections he already felt to be true.

'When I started to play the gaita I was very attracted by the technique of the Irish uilleann pipe players, the Scottish players, they played with that kind of ornament that we didn't have here.

There was a sort of decadence during the Franco years, and then we discovered all the recordings from Galicia that demonstrated that that technique that the Scottish and Irish musicians have, it was here also.

So on the Isle of Skye I met amazing scholars like Decker Forrest and Hugh Cheape. They know all of the history of the bagpipes and they think that the Scottish bagpipes, for example, came from earlier Atlantic bagpipes, that was something very much like the Spanish gaita.

The sea was really a corridor for thousands of years, the historians and the archaeologists tell us that yes, Celtic music was already there, the pipes were already there, so that explains many things that we felt.'

From Santiago we make the short journey to the north coast of Galicia and to the city of A Coruña. Here at the Obradoiro de Gaitas Seivane, Dónal is met by Susana Seivane, one of the leading gaita makers in Galicia. She is the latest in a long line of talented musicians from the Seivane family, an accomplished piper she is well-known for combining traditional Galician styles with more modern techniques.

As Susana explains, the gaita is the traditional instrument not only of Galicia but of neighbouring Asturias and of northern Portugal, all areas that lay claim to a Celtic Iberian heritage.

It is possible that this ancient instrument was the first to travel the Celtic Songlines from here in the south all the way to Scotland playing an important role in the establishment of

Visiting the Obradoiro de Gaitas Seivane in A Coruña.

At the Obradoiro de Gaitas Seivane.

Dónal with Susana Seivane.

The workshop of Obradoiro de Gaitas Seivane in A Coruña.

the Celtic musical culture of the Atlantic coasts of Europe.

Just a short walk from the centre of A Coruña is the tower of Hercules, a Roman lighthouse more than 1,900-years-old and still in use. In legend it is said that Hercules, the son of Zeus, felled the giant Geryon here and the lighthouse was built where he buried the head of his enemy.

The 180 foot tower is said to have replaced an even taller tower built by the Celts who once lived here in the ancient city of Brigantia. Their king, Breogán, founded the city and is said to have glimpsed the green shores of Ireland, more than 900 miles to the north from the top of the tower he built. According to the *Book of Invasions* the Gaels of Galicia set sail north and reached Ireland where they founded a new Celtic nation deposing the Tuatha Dé Danann.

Looking out over these same blue waters today you can imagine that Breogán really did catch a glimpse of those distant green shores more than 2,000 years ago, and that those Celts were the first to set sail along the Celtic Songlines.

This has been a remarkable journey and the further Dónal has travelled the more convincing it seems that the Celtic Songlines are indeed real. From the Hebrides to Galicia those constant reminders of a common Celtic past have always been evident. In language, in landscape and most of all in music there is a vibrant Celtic culture alive today on Europe's Atlantic shores.

The traditions are singular but they are part of something bigger, a common past that cannot be ignored as evidenced by the music itself.

Everywhere we have been we have felt at home and seen how the Celtic traditions of the past are helping forge new Celtic traditions of the future.

There is still is a flourishing Celtic culture stretching more than 1,000 miles along these spectacular Atlantic coasts.

Traditional Galician gaita players.

Dónal takes in the view from the top of the Tower of Hercules, A Coruña.

Dónal at the Tower of Hercules, A Coruña.

Profile – Carlos Núñez

Carlos Núñez Muñoz is perhaps the best-known musician to have emerged from the Celtic tradition in Galicia.

A talented multi-instrumentalist, renowned as a master of the Spanish gaita, he is an exceptional flute and whistle player. A musician since childhood he has been a leading light of the Celtic musical scene for more than thirty years. A regular at major festivals including the Interceltique and Celtic Connections, his early collaborations with the Chieftains led many fans to call him the 'seventh Chieftain'. Classically trained at the Royal Conservatory in Madrid, he has collaborated with a wide range of artists including Altan, Sharon Shannon, Sinéad O'Connor and many more, as well as featuring on Irish piper Liam O'Flynn's *The Piper's Call*.

Profile – Susana Seivane

A member of the famous Seivane family of instrument makers, Susana Seivane Hoyo was immersed in the Galician musical tradition from a young age. She comes from a long line of distinguished Galician musicians, her grandfather Xosé Seivane being a noted piper. She is at the forefront of taking traditional music of the region in new directions, having released four albums to date exploring a variety of styles and arrangements usually built around a traditional Galician core.

Filming *The Celtic Songlines* at the Tower of Hercules, A Coruña.

A regular at major Celtic festivals she has collaborated with the Breton pipe band Bagad Kemper on their 2003 album *Sud-Ar Su* and toured with them throughout 2004.

A genre-crossing artist she is as at home playing in traditional Galician 'enxebre' style, folk rock or in modern collaborations.

Recommended Listening

Ireland

Séamus Ennis: *The Return from Fingal* 1997
Ceoltóirí Chualann: *Ó Riada sa Gaiety* 1969
The Chieftains: *The Chieftains* 1964
Horslips: *Happy to Meet – Sorry to Part* 1972
Planxty: *The Well Below the Valley* 1973
The Bothy Band: *The Bothy Band* 1975
Altan: *A Horse With a Heart* 1989
Máirtín O'Connor: *Perpetual Motion* 1990
Hyper[borea]: *Gaelactica* 2003
Zoë Conway: *The Horse's Tail* 2006
Laoise Kelly: *Fáilte Uí Cheallaigh* 2015

Scotland

Flora MacNeil: *Orain Floraidh
– The Songs of Flora MacNeil* 2000
Dick Gaughan: *Handful of Earth* 1981
Capercaillie: *Crosswinds* 1987
Christine Primrose/Alison Kinnaird:
Quiet Tradition 1990
Iain MacInnes: *Tryst* 1999
Alasdair Fraser & Tony McManus:
Return to Kintail 1999
The Battlefield Band:
Leaving Friday Harbour 1999
Peatbog Fairies: *Welcome to Dun Vegas* 2003

Isle of Man

Brian Stowell: *Arraneyn* 1973
Charles Guard: *Avenging and Bright* 1991
Emma Christian: *Ta'n Dooid Cheet* 1994
The Mollag Band: *Into the Tide* 1997
King Chiaullee: *Baase Cooil Stroo* 2000
Moot: *Holdfast* 2006
Barrule: *Barrule* 2014
Mec Lir: *Not an EP* 2014

Wales

Nansi Richards: *Brenhines Y Delyn* 2010
Llio Rhydderch: *Enlli* 2002
Yr Anhrefn: *Hen Wlad fy Mamau* 1995
Fernhill: *Ca Nos* 1996
The Kilbrides: *Kilbride* 1997
Carreg Lafar: *Hyn* 1998
Robin Huw Bowen: *Hen Aelwyd* 1999
Ar Log: *Ar Log VI* 2012
Jamie Smith's Mabon: *Windblown* 2012

Cornwall

Brenda Wootton: *Carillon* 1979
Bucca: *An Tol an Pedn an Telynor* 1980
Anao Atao: *Poll Lyfans* 1998
Dalla: *A Richer Vein* 2001
Caracana: *The Banks of the Fowey* 2012
Fisherman's Friends: *One and All* 2013

Brittany

Alan Stivell:
Renaissance of the Celtic Harp 1971
Kornog: *Premiere* 1984
Bagad Kemper: *Lip Ar Maout* 1995
Denez Prigent: *Irvi* 2000
Tri Yann: *Le Pélégrin* 2001
Nolwenn Korbell: *N'eo ket echu* 2003
Sylvain Barou: *Sylvain Barou* 2012
Skilda: *Skyewalker* 2013

Galicia

Milladoiro: *Milladoiro 3* 1982
Carlos Núñez: *Brotherhood of Stars* 1996
Heiva: *Tierra de Nadie* 1998
Pancho Álvarez:
Florencio, o cego dos Vilares 1998
Luétiga: *Cántabros* 1999
Susana Seivane: *Susana Seivane* 1999
Mercedes Peón: *Isué* 2000
Muxicas: *20 anos de camiño* 2007